Voices
of us

TIM DUNLOP is a writer who lives in Naarm (Melbourne). He is a sought-after panellist and public speaker in Australia and overseas, and has written extensively on grass-roots democracy and the role of the media, as well as technology and the future of work. He runs an active Twitter feed as @timdunlop, and his popular newsletter *The Future of Everything* (on Substack) is available for subscription. *Voices of us* is his fourth book.

'Save the world, save our democracy: this book shows how maybe we can do both.' **JONATHAN GREEN**

'Tim Dunlop puts the rise of the Community Independents in its historical place – not a flash in the plan, neither the beginning nor the end of a process, but a crucial step in our democracy. This is an important and easy read for anyone wishing to understand more about how we can reclaim and reshape our politics.' **TIM HOLLO**

'Tim Dunlop provides a compelling examination of the long-term trends that led to the wave of independents being elected in the 2022 election. Rather than just treat the election in isolation, *Voices of us* shows how we got here, what it means, and crucially, highlights the powerful forces in politics and the media that will continue to try to reverse the tide.' **GREG JERICHO**

'The rise of the "Voices Of" movement has shaken the two-party system in Australia to its foundations, laying the basis for a fundamental realignment in the near future. But most of us know little about the history of the movement or about the theory of politics behind it. Tim Dunlop provides us with both an inside account of the way the movement developed, and an insightful analysis of the challenge it poses to Australia's political class.' **JOHN QUIGGIN**

'A thoughtful, provocative and historically informed analysis of the rise of the independents in the 2019 federal election. Tim Dunlop charts how we arrived at this moment, the institutional failures (and some strengths) in media, political parties and in our sense of citizenship, and the possible ways forward from here, including reconceived democratic forms. This will be an influential book.' **MARGARET SIMONS**

Voices of us

The independents' movement
transforming Australian democracy

Tim Dunlop

NEWSOUTH

For Sally and John

A NewSouth book

Published by
NewSouth Publishing
University of New South Wales Press Ltd
University of New South Wales
Sydney NSW 2052
AUSTRALIA
https://unsw.press/

© Tim Dunlop 2022
First published 2022

10 9 8 7 6 5 4 3 2 1

 A catalogue record for this book is available from the National Library of Australia

ISBN: 9781742237831 (paperback)
         9781742238630 (ebook)
         9781742239569 (ePDF)

Design Josephine Pajor-Markus
Cover design Phil Campbell
Cover image (wings) S-S-S, iStock by Getty Images

Contents

Introduction

The transformation of Australian politics, one kitchen table at time

Still there are seeds to be gathered,
and room in the bag of stars.

Ursula K. Le Guin

On 4 April 2018, I received a private message via my Facebook page:

> Hey Tim. I'm in Warringah and we're soon to
> launch our movement based on the Voices4indi
> model (kitchen table conversations etc where they
> managed to vote in Cathy McGowan and boot
> out Sofie [sic] Mirabella). We are also going to
> host events, which will include author talks …
> I'd absolutely love you to come to Warringah and
> start a new conversation about the sort of future we
> want. We are called Voices of Warringah and our
> website/social media will be launching soon …

My correspondent was Louise Hislop, founder of Voices of Warringah, and later she would also be involved with Voices of Mackellar, the neighbouring electorate a little further up the coast on Sydney's Northern Beaches. It's not often you have in your possession – let alone addressed to you – a document that could be called historical, but I think that Facebook message has a claim to the description. It not only records the origins of an influential political movement; it also captures the tentative but determined attitude that would characterise their whole approach, and most of all, the clear-eyed optimism that drove them to believe that a better politics was possible.

It was obvious to me – as it was to all those who joined the various grassroots 'Voices Of'[1] organisations around Australia – that there was something fundamentally wrong with the way our politics worked, and that mainstream political parties were a big part of the problem. To their eternal credit, ordinary-extraordinary Australians like Louise Hislop dreamed that a better way was possible, and they set out to make that happen and – I can barely believe it even as I write this – they succeeded beyond anyone's wildest expectations. On 21 May 2022, Australia voted not just for change in individual seats, but for a major realignment of the way in which our political system worked.

---

1 There is great inconsistency in the media and among the organisations themselves in how this general title is applied. Some say 'Voice of', others 'Voices for', and there are variations such as 'Voice of X', 'Voice for Y', and even 'Voices4 Z'. For convenience and consistency, I refer to the general collection of these organisations as the 'Voices Of' movement.

As 2022 began, the planet was under threat from climate change; the United States was falling into turmoil; China was aggressively asserting itself throughout the Asia–Pacific; we were still dealing with the effects of a pandemic which had not just messed with our health but with how we worked and how we purchased the necessities of life (especially toilet paper); and we saw Russia launch a war in Ukraine, a reminder of the fragility of the international order, including the economic supply chains that kept us all clothed and fed. We were wearing masks, and desperately seeking RATs, and theories of society most of us thought had disappeared with the defeat of the Nazis in 1945 were gaining a new lease on life. Frightened and frightening men's groups and their gurus were violently trying to re-establish total control over women and their bodies, winding back generations of feminist victories. Even transformative moments, like the success of the equal marriage plebiscite, were being undermined by a new wave of anti-trans hatred, that, shamefully, would be weaponised by Scott Morrison himself during the election.

By the start of 2022, the Liberal–National Party Coalition was moving into its tenth year in office. Labor, having lost the so-called unlosable election of 2019, was doing its best to make themselves invisible, living in terror of what the Murdoch press might say about any policy they happened to come up with. The polls said Labor was well ahead, but nobody trusted the polls anymore, polling being another of the institutions we had lost faith in. Besides, for many, Labor was hardly an inspiring alternative.

Beyond all this, technology was changing how we worked, how we got our news, how we talked to each other, and it seemed constant surveillance was the price we had to pay to participate in anything from online shopping to watching the news on iView. Wages had been stagnant for years, and the Australian government had admitted this was as much by design on their part as it was to do with underlying productivity. And it was even worse for those outside the workforce. In a moment of we-are-all-in-this-together during the pandemic, welfare payments were lifted and nearly everyone living in official poverty was lifted out of that poverty, and for one, shining moment, it looked like it would stay that way. But then the new payments were withdrawn and we, as a nation, returned all those people to the poverty from which the pandemic payments had rescued them. It was what Associate Professor Elise Klein from the ANU called 'policy-induced poverty.' Was this really the future the land of the fair go saw for itself?

It was certainly the future Scott Morrison embraced, and let's take a moment to consider the prime minister himself, as he was then.

The problems confronting the country were institutional – they were deeply etched in how we had structured the economy and our politics – but Scott Morrison came to embody all their worst aspects. He was a walking, talking (endlessly talking) model of everything that made us uneasy about the direction in which the country was heading. It went beyond unpopularity to something more visceral, a feeling so intense that his own campaign knew there were large numbers of electorates around the country he could not visit for fear of further suppressing the Liberal Party vote. It was an extraordinary situation, especially given that it had not always been like that. For a while, the country had been in thrall to Scott Morrison, and it felt like his reign might be eternal. He looked to have mastered the art of happy-clappy governance, breezing through his role with all the ease of the salesman he was.

He certainly had the media where he wanted them.

His avalanche approach to interviews and press conferences, where he spoke seemingly without breath for minutes at a time, along with his absolute willingness in the moment to call up down and black white, left journalists reeling. They rarely laid a glove on him. He talked over them and through them and told them he didn't accept the premise of their questions, and they failed in performing their most basic duty of holding a prime minister to account. He also swamped the mainstream media and social media with carefully constructed images of himself being a regular bloke, building cubby houses, going to the footy, and, most of all, endlessly, making curries. When he wasn't performing the role of daggy dad, we were inundated with photos and videos of him projecting a martial arrogance, striding down a red carpet laid out for him on the tarmac where his RAAF jet had deposited him, and saluting lines of soldiers as if he were the commander-in-chief.

The trouble was, there was no there there, and this became increasingly apparent as his prime ministership developed. When he decided to holiday in Hawaii while the country burned over the Christmas and New Year of 2019–20, declaring that he didn't hold a hose, the spell was broken, and that phrase became his political epitaph.

The bottom line was that it felt like the world we knew was falling apart, the world we wanted was out of reach, and the head of our government was all show and no substance. We were looking for something better, and even as that something emerged from the teal mists of the Liberal Party heartland in the form of the Voices Of movement, many doubted that a bunch of women in the leafy suburbs was really going to save us. Could a political movement that began modestly in an electorate around Albury-Wodonga reinvigorate the entire body politic? Was there enough belief left in people that they might find a way to say, enough, we aren't going to put up with this anymore?

Well, change happens slowly, then it happens fast.

The Voices Of organisations, and all the sister organisations that sprang up between the elections of 2019 and 2022, built a movement, and the candidates came: Zali Steggall, Sophie Scamps, Kylea Tink, Zoe Daniels, Allegra Spender, Monique Ryan, Kate Chaney. The media christened them 'the teals' – an allusion to them being from blue (Liberal) electorates and having green politics – and it became a controversial designation: chromatically inaccurate, and with an air of dismissal about it that undermined the seriousness of their mission, the importance of their grassroots origins, and the fact that they were, indeed, independents, not members of a 'teal' party. Eventually the name took on a more positive ring – especially when they won. Against all odds, against some of the biggest names in the modern Liberal Party, against a sometimes vicious media campaign, and a dirty, corflute-tearing ground game run by their increasingly desperate opponents, they won.

The election result of 21 May 2022, and more importantly, the way the independents went about building their support, was a significant development in the practice of Australian politics. It delivered us the right to be optimistic after years in which politicians had lost touch with the people who conferred them with democratic legitimacy. Community organisations popped up in electorates across the country – Voices of Kooyong, Voices of Goldstein, Voices of Gilmore, Voices of Hughes, Voices of Mackellar – and they turned into something extraordinary: a reinvigorated democracy that stepped outside the constraints of the two-party system that had dominated Australian politics since World War II. They were a grassroots movement reinventing the sort of country we could be. They were, in many ways, the voices of us.

In what follows, it should be clear that I am an unabashed fan of the community processes the independents deployed in the lead-up to the election. I am also happy we have had a change of government, and that Labor have been diligent in picking off the low-hanging fruit of democratic renewal ignored by the previous government – everything from the release of the Murugappan family back to Biloela in Queensland, to the dropping of charges against East Timor whistle-blower Bernard Collaery, to

7

the abolition of the Australian Building and Construction Commission (ABCC). But I temper my approval with a fear that unless we improve the integrity of our major institutions, enhance our ability to implement practical, evidence-based solutions to all the problems that confront us, and do all this in a way that involves as many community voices as possible, while sharing the spoils of success as equally as possible, then what awaits us is an antipodean version of the democratic collapse already playing out in America.

The central thought of this book is that the only way we will achieve all of this is if the community organisations that put a record number of representatives on the crossbench in 2022 continue to grow and prosper so that we are never again held hostage to a moribund two-party system. In her opening speech to parliament, the new member for Goldstein in Melbourne, Zoe Daniels, quoted Vida Goldstein, the woman her electorate was named for: 'Study has convinced me that party government is a system that is entirely out of date … It is a cumbersome, unbusinesslike method of running the country.' What was true in the early 20th century when Goldstein wrote those words is even truer now. We are a diverse and complex nation of 25 million people, and 25 million simply doesn't go into two. Approaches to issues such as constitutional recognition of First Nations people as the next step towards a formal treaty, the liberation of women from the strictures of patriarchy, and the inevitable challenges of climate change are not the province of a single party or organisation. No single party can provide all the answers, and we should build a politics that allows diverse views to be heard, not mandates to be imposed.

The election result of 21 May 2022 gave us some breathing space, but it was the beginning of a process of reform, not the end, and to capitalise on the opportunity we have created, we need to think about our country differently. In particular, we need to discard the idea of Australia being 'the lucky country'. The author of that phrase, Donald Horne, has said that 'When I invented the phrase in 1964 to describe Australia … I didn't mean that it had a lot of material resources, [I meant that] in the lucky style we have never "earned" our democracy. We simply went along with some British habits.' Australians have been stuck with this concept ever since and it has done more harm than good to the ways in which we think about our politics and ourselves as a nation. Even Horne himself came to recognise the problems with it and complained that 'I have had to sit through the most appalling rubbish as successive generations misapplied this phrase', and I would argue that the blame belongs to more than those who 'misapplied' it and to the phrase itself.

The problem is, whether you invoke the concept of 'luck' ironically or literally, you invite a national infantilisation that is unhealthy in the extreme, one that hides the way in which power operates. To say we didn't earn our democracy is to be dangerously dismissive of the effort and challenge people faced in building a viable society: yes, it is trivially true that Australians were 'lucky' to be able to draw on the British model, but there was no guarantee that it would work in the way that it did. At every step in the process, we made choices, including incorporating aspects of the American system into ours, and it seems to me healthier that we take responsibility for those choices, the good and the tragic, rather than invoke 'luck'.

The same is true of what happened in the lead-up to the 2022 election.

The origins of the Voices Of movement are to be found in the kitchen table meetings organised by the Victorian Women's Trust in the late 1990s, and, as we shall see, these were a response to the increasing inequality and power imbalances emerging in Australia. Those gatherings, and the Voices Of movement they inspired, represented a concerted effort by citizens to respond to problems they wanted to address, and it should be clear that their success was well and truly earned. As Mary Crooks from the Victorian Women's Trust (VWT) has said, Cathy McGowan's victory in Indi in 2013 was not a fluke but 'a carefully-constructed, structured campaign'.

What Australia achieved on 21 May 2022 was done *on purpose*, and it is long past time that we expelled the whole notion of luck from our political vocabulary. It has little explanatory power and it undermines the genuine achievements we have made.

Australia can be a petty and an unadventurous place, but it is also a place of great democratic innovation that retains a self-belief inflected with egalitarianism, and the Voices Of movement is the latest attempt – and one of the most successful – to reconfigure the nation along those lines. If we don't acknowledge these successes, we make it too easy for the powerful, the broad political class, to dismiss it all as *luck* and carry on as if nothing significant has changed. We shouldn't let them get away with that sleight of hand.

This book is divided into three sections, and in each, I spell out the key events that got us to the change that happened on 21 May 2022. My task is not to tell the story of every electorate, as incredible as some of those stories are. Instead, I want to look at the way in which dissatisfaction with our political system had been growing since the economic reforms of the early 1980s and how this was the origin of the kitchen table approach that is at the heart of the Voices Of movement. Then I want to offer some thoughts on how we might continue the process of democratic reform. To do all this, I thought it was important to begin the book with an account of the Voices Of movement that lets us see just how extraordinary it was, and is. I wanted to show how it grew from nothing more than the determination of a group of women (at every level, women were the driving force) to change politics in their electorates. So in the first section, 'Zali and the zeitgeist', I tell the story of how Voices of Warringah grew out of community concerns that their political leaders were failing them, and I concentrate on Louise Hislop's incredible work there, because it is emblematic of what happened across the country. I hope her story inspires others to follow her lead in coming elections.

In the second section of the book, 'How we got to 2022', there are two chapters, and in each I trace the roots of our political discontent. What I am highlighting is the link between national identity – the ways in which we think about ourselves as a nation – and the policies that governments enact that give material shape to that identity. Between 1983 and 2022, major economic and political reforms enacted by both the Labor Party and the Liberal–National Party Coalition transformed the nation and, therefore, our sense of ourselves, and you can't talk about one without considering the other: identity affects policy, and policy affects identity. Chapter 2, then – 'Insiders and outsiders' – is about where our ideas of national identity come from and how politicians manipulate them. Chapter 3, 'Beyond two-party politics and the captured state', is about the nature of institutional power in Australia and how the status quo is being challenged by a consolidating third force in our electoral politics, those sitting on the crossbench of both houses of parliament. Together, these chapters show us the soil from which the Voices Of movement grew. They show why the 2022 election became such a challenge to the two-party system that had dominated Australian politics since the 1940s.

Chapter 4, 'When the country changes: Reforming democracy for a new era', is a look ahead, and I challenge the newly elected independents – as well as the Greens and the Labor Party – to not waste this moment in our political history. In my previous books, and my writing more generally, my argument has always been that the best answer to most problems with democracy is more democracy, and that means making every institution, from the parliament down, better represent the diverse nation that Australia irreducibly is, and I set out ideas on how that might be done. The legacy of the Morrison government and its earlier iterations has left the new Albanese government with an unenviable job of repair, but the overriding aim should be to go beyond individual policies and pursue structural reform that will bolster the democratic ballast of the nation. If we are going to manage challenges like climate change, recognition of First Nations, and gender equity – let alone all the standard and ongoing matters of economic management – we are going to need a robust democratic mindset that is reflected in our most important institutions, lest we fall into the authoritarianism already making itself felt in other parts of the world.

There's an old saying in politics that you have probably heard: never let a good crisis go to waste. It's good advice, but I think the whole point of us electing the parliament we did on 21 May 2022 was that we *avoided* a crisis; that the country saw clearly that a re-elected Morrison government would have been a disaster for Australian democracy, and so we chose something better (and how subsequent revelations have borne out the wisdom of that choice!). We did that, not by luck, but by using the tools made available to us by Australia's unique democratic system, and it is now up to us to build on what we have created.

This book is about how groups of concerned citizens

– groups overwhelmingly led by women – managed with joy, determination and focus to develop a movement that rewrote the political rule book. It is about how they faced down the anger, frustration and sense of foreboding about Australia's future that had been building over decades and, with a practical model of community participation, changed the nation one kitchen table at a time. It is also about what we must do next to make sure these changes are bedded down so that we can move towards being the sort of progressive, open, economically stable and egalitarian nation many of us want Australia to be. It is about making sure that the opportunity the election of 21 May has offered us doesn't slip away as the forces of the status quo relentlessly try to regain control.

If all of this sounds too wildly optimistic to be true, then so be it.

For too long, we have let the cynicism inherent in business-as-usual politics obliterate our sense that something better is possible. We have let a mainstream political media that has lost its sense of purpose define our democracy in a narrow and nasty way. And we have let outdated notions of national identity shape our country in ways that are no longer appropriate.

It's time for something better.

Part One
Zali and the zeitgeist

Cathy McGowan went forth, not with a list of issues from a consultation. She went forth as the voice of the people. She knew that she was standing there expressing what people had said. And I think that made a huge difference because they heard themselves in Cathy's voice and they were ready to go with her.

Alana Johnson, co-founder, Voice4Indi

1

Experts for means.
Citizens for ends.

Persuasion is not possible without appeal to either experiences or desires, in other words to immediate political needs.

Hannah Arendt

The election of 21 May 2022 was not a clash of parties and candidates in the usual way. It wasn't even a clash of ideologies as we normally understand that concept in politics. What it presented us with was a contest of methodologies, between a bottom-up and a top-down understanding of political representation. Whereas mainstream politics and the major parties focused on elections and competition between rivals, the Voices Of movement was about the space *between* elections; about ongoing consultation at a local level, conducted in a spirit of co-operation. The 21 May election pitted professional politicians against independent candidates, which was another way of saying that it pitted those obliged to put the needs of a party first against locals who just wanted to get things done for their communities.

Most importantly, the methodology deployed by the independents who ran in 2022 was based on listening, not telling, and it is crucial to understand that. Their approach was about opening the conversation as widely as possible, moving it out from behind the closed doors and limited guest lists of the mainstream media and the other spaces dominated by the usual suspects. What people wanted was not *bipartisanship* between major parties, but a bigger table at which many voices were able to have a seat and a say. People wanted to wield political power on behalf of their own communities, not on behalf of a party.

In all these ways, the 2022 federal election was a contest of outsiders against insiders, and against all odds, the outsiders won. Or rather, they made enormous strides towards normalising their methodology of engagement, based on listening and co-operation. The challenge that remains for all of us who support the democratic advances made on 21 May is to invest the institutions of the state with the same processes of engagement and co-operation. To do that, we need to understand the origins and power of the Voices Of methodology.

What happened on 21 May 2022 is generally traced to the successful campaign Cathy McGowan ran in Indi in regional Victoria in 2013, but it is important to recognise that McGowan and her team worked with another group of women whose methodology of engagement with communities reached back into the 1990s. In her memoir, *Cathy Goes to Canberra*, McGowan speaks about the way in which this came about, saying

that she and Alana Johnson, another member of the
nascent Voice4Indi organisation, began planning their
approach during a work trip to India together:

> Alana was already active in Voices for Indi as
> were a couple of other women on the trip. As we
> travelled around by bus, we workshopped how to
> run a community engagement program around
> politics in north-eastern Victoria. By the time
> we got back from India, we had designed a clear
> process for the implementation of what became
> known as kitchen table conversations. The kitchen
> table conversations model built on community
> engagement work done by the Victorian Women's
> Trust as part of the Purple Sage and Watermark
> projects, in which many members of Australian
> Women in Agriculture had participated.

Cathy McGowan is rightly hailed as a central figure in
the rise of the independents' movement, but we should
not underestimate the role played by the Victorian
Women's Trust, and Mary Crooks, its executive director
for 25 years. Crooks was the driving force behind the
Purple Sage project that McGowan mentions. It began in
August 1998 and brought together six organisations: the
Victorian Women's Trust (VWT); the Stegley Found-
ation; the Brotherhood of St Laurence; the Victorian
Local Governance Association; the People Together
Project; and the YWCA Victoria. It was instigated, as they
record in a report available on the VWT website, because

they were 'increasingly concerned about developments in Victoria at the time', including 'a widening gap between the rich and the poor, continued high unemployment, reduced standards of community service, increased strain on local communities (particularly in regional Victoria), the loss of public assets, racism and social tensions, and an erosion of our democratic rights and culture'.

In other words, their concerns were with the consequences of the neoliberal turn I describe in the next chapter, though at the time of Purple Sage, 'neoliberalism' wasn't the expression that was used: people tended to talked about 'free market economics' or 'economic rationalism', which the Purple Sage report described as an approach whereby 'government must pull back and play a less interventionist role, and, as a matter of priority, scale back its expenditure.' They also noted that this new system enshrined 'competition as a governing principle in all public policy'.

It is simply stunning as you read this history how often you see people express concerns with the direction in which the country was going under these changed economic conditions, and you realise the forces that drove the transformation that came to pass on 21 May 2022 were hiding in plain sight the whole time. Dissatisfaction with the economic reforms of the 1980s, and with the status quo more generally, was deep-seated and spread across classes, and people knew in their bones that something was wrong with the direction we were heading. One of the Purple Sage participants said that the 'economic rationalist approach currently being taken by our governments ... fails to respect our environment or those many individuals who contribute to the common good in other than commercially measurable ways', and these were concerns you were likely hear expressed at any kitchen table discussion run by the Voices Of organisations in the run-up to the 2022 election.

Technological change was altering the material conditions of life, throwing up challenges around the nature of work, and changing the fundamental character of Australian life. Just as importantly, we were moving away from the model of male-dominated industries and towards ones in which women were much more prominent and were, rightly, demanding their voices and concerns be heard in a way that the major parties, the Liberals in particular, were failing to do. Perhaps it is not surprising, then, that Purple Sage was led by women, and that nearly all the Voices Of candidates have been women too. Just as importantly, the support teams behind them have nearly all been women – it is women all the way down – and this represented a sea change in the world of Australian politics, reflecting deeper changes in society that are worth noting.

The single biggest category of workers in Australia is now professional women, while the number of women in the caring trades outstripped the number of men in more traditional trades as far back as 2015. Journalist and researcher George Megalogenis pointed out in an article in the *Sydney Morning Herald* that the key 'teal' seats, 'as well as Perth's wealthiest seat of Curtin and two Liberal seats in Adelaide – Boothby and Sturt' all have 'above-average shares of female voters, with Kooyong ranked highest of the group at 52.6 per cent – more than a percentage point above the national total of 51.2 per cent'.

All this lent momentum to the involvement of women in the political process, but the Voices Of methodology itself, first developed by Mary Crooks and the Victorian Women's Trust, *encouraged* the emergence of women. The bottom-up, listening-to methodology they employed deliberatively targeted barriers that women and other outsiders faced in these environments, creating safe spaces in which they could speak and be listened to and have their views taken seriously. These elements came together and created a political earthquake, the consequences of which will rumble through the next election and beyond.

Mary Crooks became involved with Voice4Indi after an invitation from Alana Johnson. Crooks told Margo Kingston in a 2021 podcast interview that the kitchen table conversations were driven by women and that, 'without getting too highbrow about it, its feminism lies in women's preferred ethic which I think is to co-operate and collaborate' and that 'it's an antidote to the command-and-control kind of culture that we are saturated in across a patriarchal world.' She noted that 'the overwhelming majority of table hosts, or group leaders, have been women … up around 87 per cent of our group', and that 'what tends to happen is that women have the energy and the capacity to start this process and they tend to bring the men in and that's what has happened.'

The formal engagement between Voice4Indi and Mary Crooks began in October 2012, and as Crooks explained, they 'sat around the table and they told me about Voices and what their objectives were, and their question was whether or not the Women's Trust model could be adapted and tailored to an electorate.' They decided it could, and Crooks returned to Indi in November to further the process. It was then, Crooks and Alana Johnson explained, that they came up against internal tensions involving a clash of styles between the men and women participants. The men just wanted to choose a candidate and get on with it, but as Johnson pointed out, this missed an important step in the process.

> We knew this was a process that had to give people a way to reclaim their rightful democratic voice, and that wasn't going to happen by just standing an independent candidate. That would not change at all how people perceive their connection to politics. All they would have was somebody else to vote for in a system that still silenced them. That candidate might have been preferred, but it was never going to fundamentally change the relationship.

Crooks saw the same problem.

'There was quite a palpable tension visible to me as an outsider,' she said of the second Indi gathering, 'that women in particular felt very strongly about the need to engage community authentically, and, with great respect, the blokes as a general rule, despite their passion and enthusiasm, they were sort of tapping the table and rolling their eyes a little bit because they just wanted to flesh out a candidate and go for it.'

Crooks put her foot down and told them that they 'needed to resolve this, and the best way of resolving it was to put all of their energies and capacity into designing a process across the electorate.'

'The thing is,' Crooks said, 'when you get a group of committed and capable people around the table, you don't need multiple degrees. It's not rocket science, but it has to be done properly and thoughtfully.' And this is crucial. The Voices Of methodology takes politics back into the realm of the everyday and hands control to the community. This doesn't mean that you are not going to need expert advice around policy development and implementation; it means that, in terms of what you want out of a political process, ordinary voters are as well-equipped as anyone to provide input. In fact, they need to be central to the process. So the bottom line is, you need both: citizens in general, whose goals are the entire point of democratic politics and the source of its legitimacy; and then, ultimately, a range of experts and specialists who can deploy that expertise in pursuit of citizens' goals.

Experts for means. Citizens for ends.

The formulation presumes a shared competence and a common destiny.

There is crossover – the experts will themselves be citizens – but the point is the role each plays in the democratic process. The relationship is not inherently competitive, certainly not in the way that a two-party political system leads us to believe. If anything, the relationship is co-operative, but only if you have institutional arrangements in place that allow co-operation rather than competition. And where competition inevitably arises, you need to have mechanisms that allow that competition to be resolved internally – within the institutions themselves – rather than being projected back onto the community in the form of culture wars and other disputations that inevitably (and often by design) lead to polarisation and conflict.

A key to the methodology Crooks and others developed, then, was that once the process of listening was in place – the kitchen table conversations and other gatherings – organisers had to report back to the participants, demonstrating to them that they had been listened to. 'Absolutely fundamental,' Crooks said, and she explained why. 'Everybody who participated – everybody – needs to have a sense that what they said and what their group said has actually been taken into account', and that the reporting process distils what was said 'faithfully and with rigour.' This happened in Indi, and when the report was done, Cathy McGowan had what Crooks called 'this extraordinary authentic platform from which to speak … this incredible platform of community voice. She knew it. She understood it. She got it, and she worked beautifully with it.'

Another founding member of Voice4Indi was Denis Ginnivan, who now travels the country helping other groups do what he and the Indi team did prior to the

2013 federal election (as does Cathy McGowan). He told Margo Kingston and Peter Clarke in another podcast interview that 'there's no one formula' for such local groups, but that 'the key elements are that they start out with a group of people who are yearning to do something about politics.' He said that whatever form the organisation takes, there must be a common sense of purpose, so that it isn't just a bunch of people sitting around talking politics, but a goal-directed group that has 'a constituted structure' where there is 'one common statement of purpose' and that 'they all agree what it is about and what it isn't about.' With such a structure comes accountability, and that is the key.

The transformative nature of this approach lies in the fact that its spirit of community and co-operation will extend into the practice of politics itself, and it certainly permeated McGowan's approach once she was elected, even in the hotbed of the Canberra parliament. Writing an early account of her arrival on the scene for the *Inside Story* website, journalist Brett Evans noted that even her staff didn't fit the standard-issue model of political staffer:

> My guide to McGowan's office is a neatly turned-out schoolteacher, Prue Noble, once a foot soldier in the Indi insurgency. As we walk together across a glassed-in bridge, I'm reminded once again that you can tell a lot about politicians by their staff ... There are the press secretaries who plonk their tape recorder down next to yours (with the unspoken

accusation that you can't be trusted to quote their boss accurately) or the personal assistants who are far too busy waiting for the phone to ring to offer you a cup of tea.

But Prue, I soon find out, is a chatty, unjaded outsider – and a volunteer. Over the next three years, she explains, McGowan intends to rotate as many ordinary Voice for Indi people through her Canberra office as she can. In this way, she hopes hundreds of locals will get to experience first-hand national politics from the vantage point of an MP's office.

As huge a step as it was when McGowan was elected to parliament in 2013 and began modelling a different approach to politics, vindicating the bottom-up approach Voice4Indi had taken, there was still a question mark over what would happen next. Was this all a one-off fluke embodied in the perhaps impossible-to-replicate attributes that Cathy McGowan brought to the job, or was it possible to make the process survive and prosper in such a way that its benefits were transferable to a new candidate?

These questions were, in part, answered when McGowan ran again in 2016 and not only won but increased her majority. The real test, however, came at the election after that, in 2019, by which time McGowan had announced her retirement, and Voices for Indi (as it was now known) had found a replacement candidate in Helen Haines, a nurse and midwife who also had a background in researching rural health care. She grew up on a dairy farm in Colac, Victoria, and she lived with her husband, an agricultural scientist, and their three children on a small farm near Wangaratta.

McGowan's memoir begins with the tension – terror – she felt as the early count began rolling in on election night in 2019, with the first booths showing a tight result, and she spoke of her concern about whether she would be able to 'pass the baton':

> There had been many independent Members of Parliament through the years but once they surrendered their seats, they were replaced by candidates from political parties. What we were aiming for in 2019 was a first: a handover from one independent to another. Voices for Indi – we changed the name, adding the 's' in 2014 … is not a political party, and this time our candidate was Helen Haines, who, like me, had deep and extensive ties throughout our region …
>
> By 8.30 pm Helen was still in it. But we could see that there was an unexpected swing nationally to the Morrison government … Then came a result from one of the polling places in Mansfield, historically deep blue, a reliably Liberal-voting town, although we'd managed to win it in 2016. If we could put on a decent showing there, we'd probably go on to win. Someone from Mansfield called out the result: Helen had held on. The crowd erupted.

McGowan writes that not only had they done politics 'in a way that we wanted, but we'd staved off yet another fierce campaign in the electorate by the Liberal Party. The people in our community had made a decision that they didn't want to hand back their power to a political party. They wanted something bigger and better: to be directly involved in how their local member would represent them in the federal parliament.'

Everybody involved in subsequent Voices Of organisations agrees that this was a turning point. Denis Ginnivan has said that Haines's victory in 2019 was central to his having the confidence to offer the Indi model to other jurisdictions. He told Kingston and Clarke that after Haines won it was clear that 'this idea wasn't just a brush off, a one-off opportunity that went away again. It was actually an idea that had merit and prospects for continuity.' What they had learnt was that when you take people in communities seriously, giving them the tools to address their own concerns, they will rise to the challenge.

The next major turning point was the election of Zali Steggall in Warringah on Sydney's Northern Beaches in 2019, but it is important to realise that the Steggall moment depended on legwork that went back at least to the previous election (2016), and it is worth tracing what happened, particularly the role played by Louise Hislop, the family business owner who founded Voices for Warringah. Hislop's wake-up call, she has explained, was when she heard journalist Margo Kingston speak during the 2004 promotional tour for Kingston's book

Not Happy, John. Kingston not only spelled out for the audience of which Hislop was a part the ways in which she thought Australian democracy was slipping away from ordinary people, she challenged them do something about it.

'I put those words in my back pocket. I stewed on them. I read the book. I ruminated,' Hislop wrote in a later account of the moment on the *No Fibs* website. In fact, Hislop's story is studded with moments and realisations that many Voices Of participants speak of, from the candidates up, realisations that also inspired the kitchen table conversation methodology of Mary Crooks: frustration about the direction in which the country was going; the realisation that people in power were taking them for granted and not listening to their concerns; the feeling that the Liberal Party in particular had gone so far to the right that there was no place for what people like Hislop saw as their own combination of fiscal conservatism and social progressivism; and the realisation that climate change was being ignored. Often these concerns manifested for them in the person of their local member.

Hislop's local member was Tony Abbott, who in 2011 was Leader of the Opposition, and who had set about undermining the Gillard government's approach to climate change with slogans like 'Wrecking Ball to the Economy', 'Great Big New Tax', 'Whyalla Wipeout' and '$100 Lamb Roasts'. Inspired by a television ad aired by a group called 'Say Yes' – as in, say yes to a price on carbon – Hislop formed a Northern Beaches branch of

Say Yes and found herself around a table with ten friends wondering what it was they were supposed to do next. She described the scene:

> My friend Dave hands out the paper and pens, suggests the things we could write about, puts a timer on and generally takes control, much to my relief. All I have to do is ensure the tea is hot and write something. Easy! We decide to organise an event with a giant inflatable planet Earth that was travelling around the country. I volunteer to make a sign.

Eventually Hislop was put in charge of organising a Facebook page for the group, even though she didn't have a Facebook page herself and had no idea how social media worked, let alone how to use it as a campaigning tool. As we shall see, social media became vital to many aspects of these local organisations, including the Voices Of groups that eventually strode to victory in 2022, but for now, Hislop was fumbling. Her Say Yes group managed to hold a public protest at the Duke Kahanamoku statue in Freshwater, near Manly Beach, and they received some coverage in the local newspaper. This raised their level of ambition, and Dave suggested they write to Tony Abbott and ask for a meeting. Hislop was terrified at the idea but put up her hand to be part of a delegation, egged on by a mantra she had composed for herself after hearing Margo Kingston challenge her audience: *If no-one does anything, nothing is going to happen!* It was not exactly high oratory, Hislop admitted, but it worked for her. They approached Abbott about a meeting, and it took his office 14 months to respond.

When eventually they sat down with him, the meeting was civil, but Hislop was shocked at how dismissive their local member was of their concerns. She challenged him on the slogan-laden fear campaign he was running about the Gillard government's *Clean Energy Act* of 2011, pointing out that he himself had once supported a price on carbon. In her account of the meeting, Hislop says:

> He puts his hands up in front of his chest with his palms facing me, slowly shakes his head and says in his stilted way: 'Louise, Louise, you and I, we, ahh, have very different ways of looking at the world.'
>
> 'How do you know how I look at the world? You've just met me!
>
> 'Tony, I went to the same school as your daughters. I come from a Catholic family, my husband and I have a mortgage and three kids. We are small business owners and we employ five young men who live on the Northern Beaches. I am exactly the sort of person you should be representing!'
>
> It doesn't matter what I say. He doesn't feel the need to justify his position. He thinks saying we are different is all he needs to do.

In a sense it was, because after this meeting Hislop was even more determined.

Australian politics at that time, you will recall, was moving at breakneck speed. Julia Gillard, who had successfully challenged Kevin Rudd as leader of Labor and had therefore become prime minister, was under attack from Abbott and large sections of the mainstream media. It was a relentless campaign, rife with misogyny and patriarchal entitlement, that in the end produced Gillard's now-famous misogyny speech on the floor of the parliament, which remains one of the great moments of Australian political oratory and, I would argue, a moral turning point for the country. But the right wing campaign against Gillard worked, and she in turn was ousted by Kevin Rudd, who, reinstalled as prime minister, took Labor to a loss at the next federal election, the party taking solace from the fact that the reversion to Rudd had 'saved some of the furniture' – meaning that they believed the loss would have been larger under Gillard.

So now Louise Hislop's local member, Tony Abbott, was prime minister, and he quickly established himself as what many saw as one of the worst prime ministers of recent Australian history. He openly broke key election commitments, and then, on 13 May 2014, with his Treasurer, Joe Hockey, delivered an austere budget that left the country reeling. In Abbott's electorate of Warringah, there was a sense, from various accounts, that they felt a responsibility for the pain their local member, the prime minister, was inflicting on the country, and it increased the desire to find someone to challenge him for the seat of Warringah.

Hislop was now part of another local organisation, People of Warringah (PoW), who were determined to remove Tony Abbott, and they were not the only ones with plans – or at least the desire – to challenge Abbott at the next election. Another who stepped up was James Mathison, one of the hosts of the popular television program *Australian Idol*. Responding to a call-out on Twitter to find someone to run against Abbott, Mathison said he would do it. A political neophyte, he nonetheless brought star power to proceedings and was able to attract the attention of the mainstream media in a way most local campaigns were unable to do.

Hislop's Facebook page, meanwhile, was starting to grow, as was her mailing list. The *Sydney Morning Herald* published a story by Wendy Harmer about PoW, Harmer being one of the few mainstream journalists to take seriously the groups who were trying to change things at a local level, and her piece kept the momentum going.

Federal political turmoil continued, and in a mirror image of the Rudd–Gillard leadership swapsies, Tony Abbott lost an internal party ballot and was replaced as leader – and as prime minister – by Malcolm Turnbull. For Hislop and the others in Warringah, this solved one problem, but Tony Abbott was still their local member and that was not something they wanted to continue. In fact, many presumed that, having lost the leadership, and having been in parliament for more than 20 years, Abbott would resign, but that's not what happened.

So James Mathison proceeded with his challenge, and

it was a key moment in the progress of local insurgencies on their way to the election of 2022. Hislop organised to meet Mathison and offered to provide whatever help she and her various local groups could. They joined forces, but neither of them was kidding themselves about the challenge they faced. She wrote about their first meeting:

> I say: 'You know you won't win, don't you?'

> He says: 'That's okay,' and points his finger up to 12 o'clock. 'If we can just turn the dial this much (points to 2 o'clock), it will be that much easier for the next person.'

Keep your eye on that clock.

At the federal election in 2016, with a war chest of a relatively measly $15K, Mathison, Hislop and their team embarked on their David-versus-Goliath campaign. Again, Mathison's celebrity helped with mainstream exposure, and everyone from Kurt Pengilly, saxophonist and guitarist from INXS, to Tony Windsor, the New England independent who, on the floor of the house, had thrown his vote behind the Gillard government, offered support and assistance. The family grassroots came through too, and Hislop wrote:

> My nephew Sean takes photos for the website.
> My sister Kathie and daughter Madeline join
> the campaign while my husband runs our family
> business on his own. I've never worked so hard in

my life or been so pumped. Madeline and Steve take over the running of the household. They and my sister Kathie are my rocks. We call in favours from friends for graphic design, T-shirts and posters. My friend Vik makes a giant, laminated poster of a map of Warringah. We stick it on the wall. My friend Alicia has a baby and wants something to work on while she's at home – she takes charge of the admin and the ever-growing list of volunteers.

A poll emerged that suggested Mathison might just get over the line because of preferences, an idea lent substance by the fact that the local Greens candidate, Clara Williams Rolden, had announced that she would preference Mathison over the Labor candidate. This possibility was reported in a story by leading political reporter Phil Coorey, in an article in the *Australian Financial Review*, and it created concern in mainstream political circles, and unleashed a range of tactics from the major parties that would become familiar all the way through to the 2022 election: a deluge of money into the electorate, especially from the Liberal Party, and a string of attempts to smear the independent. The Labor candidate in Warringah in 2016, Andrew Woodward, was all over social media accusing Mathison of being a 'Liberal stooge', just as Liberals Josh Frydenberg, Tim Wilson, Jason Falinski and Dave Sharma would later attempt to smear their independent challengers in 2022 as 'fakes' and 'stooges'.

Most importantly, Hislop argued, Malcolm Turnbull

himself intervened, and managed to 'turn the dial'. The prime minister released a statement saying that 'A vote for your local Liberal is a vote for stable government and a plan for jobs. An Independent/Green/ALP vote means chaos. Together, let's see it through.' For many in these coastal, blue-ribbon, metropolitan electorates, Turnbull still represented the best of the Liberal Party they had grown up with, and if he was on the scene, they were willing to stick with the party.

Nonetheless, Mathison's Warringah candidacy did exactly what he had set out to do – moved the hands on the clock. Abbott suffered a swing against of him of around 9 per cent, his primary vote dropping from 60.9 per cent in 2013 to 51.65 per cent in 2016. The result showed Louise Hislop what was possible, and she redoubled her efforts, moving into the formation of Voices of Warringah and the 2019 federal election. But before that happened, she continued to hone her skills and became involved in an independent campaign at state level, after the resignation of NSW Liberal premier Mike Baird. Hislop joined Kathryn Ridge in trying to win Baird's seat, and this put in place some of the connections that would become crucial in the run-up to the 2019 federal election and beyond. Ridge was interested in the 'kitchen table' approach used by Cathy McGowan in Indi, and she invited Denis Ginnivan and Phil Haines from Voices for Indi to speak to her team. The methodology appealed strongly to Hislop too, and she made it central to her approach.

In March 2018, Hislop invited 20 people to her

house to talk about forming Voices of Warringah (VoW). In April, she contacted me about coming to speak to her new organisation, which I did in October that year, the first of many such talks the VoW team organised, with people like Father Rod Bower, Jane Caro and Richard Denniss. At the gathering I spoke with, I was struck by what a well-heeled and well-educated group they were, and I was conscious that I might have been coming at them from a position more to the left than they were comfortable with. I mean, I was. But I also sensed a willingness to listen and learn, and an overwhelming sense of the need they felt to rid themselves of Tony Abbott. The anger at his neglect, his failure as PM, and his ongoing unwillingness to engage, particularly on climate change, was palpable, and it was clear to me, and I wrote at the time, that if they could find the right candidate, that person would be in with a decent chance of unseating him.

The zeitgeist was humming. But none of this was easy.

Uncharacteristically, and out of obvious concern about his declining local popularity, Abbott organised a community meeting, and Hislop went along. Her question to him was greeted with groans from the mainly male audience, as well as outright dismissal from Abbott himself. He told everyone of her involvement with the Mathison campaign, and dismissively repeated what he had said when he met her in his office: if you don't like me, don't vote for me. But Hislop gave as good as she got, and told him and the audience that, 'not only will I not vote for you, I will ensure anyone else who does not agree with your radically conservative views and actions will not vote for you either!'

She was defiant, but despair was creeping in too, and she texted James Mathison that night: 'I feel so alone, anxious, unsupported, out of my depth, abandoned and overwhelmed.'

Then, in the way of these things – where the tiny snowball you've sent rolling down the hill starts to gain size and momentum – Hislop was contacted out of the blue by Julie Gianessini, a former member of the Liberal Party, who introduced Hislop to an organisation that called itself the Coalition of the Willing (CoW), another one of the local groups that had sprung up in this blue-ribbon electorate. Through CoW, Hislop met 'Andy' from Manly Vale, and a mother of four from Seaforth on the Northern Beaches. The woman was an events organiser, and Andy had IT skills, and Hislop started to feel like she was gathering a team around her who had the tools they needed to get things done. Denis Ginnivan held another seminar in the area called 'Getting Elected to Represent Your Community', and at this event Hislop was introduced to Gabrielle Chan, a journalist from *Guardian Australia*, one of the mainstream journalists who took the Voices Of movement seriously long before her peers in the industry.

Chan's article, 'Tony Abbott faces campaign using tactics that defeated Mirabella in Indi', set in motion a new wave of interest in what Hislop and others were doing, and it was another life-changing moment for

Hislop herself. The article and the publicity it brought – everything from retweets on Twitter by the likes of Alex Turnbull, son of the prime minister, to endless interviews for Hislop herself – saw the creation of more local groups. They were all dedicated not just to the removal of Tony Abbott as member for Warringah but to consciousness-raising and a desire for action on one issue in particular: climate change.

CoW and VoW were joined in the field by the likes of Think Twice Warringah, run by local schoolteacher Daniel Moller, as well as an offshoot of CoW that would become known as Big Coalition of the Willing, or Big CoW, meaning CoW itself would henceforth be referred to by those involved as Small CoW. A group called 'Let's not re-elect Tony Abbott' – you have to love the clarity of these names – came into existence, and it attracted the attention and vocal support of Layne Beachley, the seven-time surfing world champion who lived in the electorate. She released a public statement condemning Abbott's hostility to the very idea of climate change and she made the matter local: 'We need a leader who is open to protecting and preserving our coastlines and natural resources,' Beachley said in her statement.

Another group, Stop Adani Warringah, also formed, and it was a further manifestation of local concern about climate change more generally. Even GetUp! got involved in the campaign against Tony Abbott, although they had previously declined a request by Hislop to do so on the grounds that removing him was an impossible task and not worth their resources. Their belated arrival on the scene was a measure of the success Hislop and the various groups had been having, and although Hislop and her team didn't know it at the time, the national zeitgeist was working in their favour too.

After a number of leadership spills within the Liberal Party, Malcolm Turnbull was replaced as party leader and prime minister on 24 August 2018. When the spills began two days earlier, it looked as if his successor would be Peter Dutton, but Dutton eventually lost to Scott Morrison. Turnbull subsequently retired from parliament, and on 20 October 2018, a by-election for his seat of Wentworth was held in Sydney's Eastern suburbs. Turnbull's retirement appeared strategic, and was one of many actions he would take that would give momentum to non-Liberal candidates. He would not endorse Dave Sharma, the person the Liberals pre-selected to replace him, and right up to the election of 2022, he let it be known that he supported many of the independent candidates who were emerging. (Even as I write this, rumours continue to reach me that Turnbull is investigating the possibility of forming a new centre-right party.)

Wentworth, like Warringah, was about as safe a Liberal seat as you could find – in fact, the single richest electorate in the country – but anger was so acute at the way the party had treated Turnbull that they voted for the independent, Dr Kerryn Phelps, the former head of the Australian Medical Association (AMA). She pulled off this win with an incredible swing of just under 20 per cent, the first time since the seat came into existence in

1901 that it had not been held by the Liberals or one of the earlier iterations of that party.

Up until the announcement of the Wentworth by-election, Phelps had been planning to run for Lord Mayor of Sydney, but her supporters saw an opportunity and convinced her to switch. And although she didn't explicitly establish a Voices Of–type organisation, her team adopted similar strategies of local engagement. Phelps's team was professional, with businesswoman and activist Wendy McCarthy as campaign chair; Darrin Barnett, who had worked on Julia Gillard's campaign; and Anthony Reed, another former Labor adviser with campaign experience. But Phelps also worked with the local community. She has said that once word was out that her campaign was under way, 'people just started turning up. They told us what their skill set was and they went to work.' She has also said that 'most of the time we were just winging it' and that 'I spoke at candidate forums, held press conferences, stood at train stations and ferry stops. We doorknocked as much as we could. We had to do a lot of listening and a lot of talking.'

Phelps's victory, when it happened, was wind in the sails for those campaigning to remove Tony Abbott on the other side of the harbour in Warringah, and in fact this was the moment that things got serious for Louise Hislop and Voices of Warringah. She decided to leave the organisation she had formed – confident it was in good, local hands – so she could concentrate on the campaign itself. What's more, those working with Hislop realised that they needed to move onto a more professional footing, as Phelps had, and her campaign manager, Anthony Reed, came on board in Warringah. Dof Dickinson, who was head of the international marketing and strategy agency Brains, also joined the campaign.

I asked Hislop what the difference was between the campaign proper and Voices of Warringah, and she stressed that it was important to realise that they were entirely separate entities and fulfilled very different roles. 'The campaign was a professional team of people managing everything. We had an events coordinator; we had a fundraising co-ordinator; we had a media person; we had me running the whole show; we had Anthony as the strategy advisor. We had a communications person, and an operations person. We had someone dealing with ordering all the pamphlets that you make up during the campaign, and the T-shirts, and that's a big job doing that kind of thing. So the campaign was where the actual work was done.'

The campaign, Hislop said, also involved fundraising and the spending of the money that was raised. She said it is 'a big job to work out where and what to spend the money on, and then the actual spending is very time-consuming. There's a lot of messaging, there's a lot of artwork, there's a lot of quotes to get in and consider. And then there's newsletters that go out to the whole community. It's a lot of work on a professional campaign like this. And that's the difference. I mean, Voices of Warringah and Vote Tony Out weren't doing any of that stuff. But what they did added to our success.'

Voices of Warringah specifically chose not to search for a candidate, out of a deeply held belief that that was not their role. Candidates were to emerge from the process of local engagement, rather than being imposed by any one organisation. Nonetheless, by this point a candidate was needed, and the campaign, of which Hislop was now part, had some key criteria. 'Our ideal person,' Hislop told me, 'was someone with a high profile, and who was a professional woman.' Small CoW was actively fielding applications, but it was another local group, Vote Tony Out, that eventually unearthed the candidate from central casting, Zali Steggall. She wasn't just a local barrister, she was the first Australian ever to win a Winter Olympics gold medal, and a much-loved local. Hislop was part of the small team that initially spoke with Steggall to assess her suitability and Hislop says that, after sitting at a kitchen table (where else?) with Steggall and her husband Tim, she came away inspired, saying, 'I realised at that moment we could win.'

The identity of the new candidate was kept secret until the day of the press conference, which was held on Australia Day, 26 January 2019. Even locals had been kept in the dark, but the multifarious community groups had worked the phones and their email lists to ensure there was a sizeable turnout for the event at the North Harbour Reserve. The launch attracted mainstream media attention too, and inevitably, once the candidate was revealed as Zali Steggall, it turned into a major news story.

In the meantime, kitchen table conversations were happening all over the electorate, and one often spawned several others as participants were inspired to run their own. Hislop and her team began training volunteers for the campaign and the key message they imparted was: be prepared, be positive and be polite. This became the motto for Team Zali. They also divided the team into local groups, and discrete organisations began working specific areas, such as the Lower North Shore crew run by Kirsty Gold, one of the original members of Small CoW, and Tina Jackson, also an early supporter. Both had been, Hislop knew, lifelong Liberal voters.

Momentum at this stage was building – overflowing – but they knew that winning the election was still going to be an incredible challenge. The Liberal Party started throwing everything they had at the electorate, as did the Murdoch media. The *Daily Telegraph* made much of the involvement of GetUp! in the campaign to remove Abbott – seeing, or concocting, left-wing conspiracies, a tactic that would be used against all the independents going into the 2022 federal election. The right-wing version of GetUp!, Advance Australia, showed up on the streets of Warringah in vans emblazoned with billboards that said, 'Vote Steggall, Get Shorten'.

By the time the election was announced on 11 April 2019 – to be held on 18 May, just over five weeks later – Team Zali was running like clockwork and there was an air of confidence. The 'three Ps' were being observed by the growing team of volunteers – prepared, positive, polite – and they were easily holding the line against everything Tony Abbott, the Liberal Party and the Murdoch media were ranging against them.

The key moment was a one-on-one debate between Tony Abbott and Zali Steggall organised by Sky News and hosted by David Speers. It was clear that Abbott supporters would be out in force at the venue for the debate, the Queenscliff Surf Club, looking to encourage any sort of confrontation with Team Zali that the cameras of assembled media might catch, and Hislop and her team decided to abandon their, by now, well-known turquoise (not teal!) Zali T-shirts, and to allow only those among their team with a ticket for the event to attend. It had the desired effect, catching the primed Abbott supporters flat-footed, and the hoped-for confrontation was avoided.

During the debate, Steggall not only held her own, she took the fight up to the much more experienced Abbott and caught him out on key issues, to the extent that at one point he said that he was sick of listening to experts, a remark that set the studio audience laughing. By election day, Hislop was as sure as she could be that they had it in the bag – every indicator said so – and indeed, as they sat in a room at the local Novotel hotel watching the election coverage on the ABC, Warringah was the first seat election analyst Antony Green called, announcing that Zali Steggall had won, and won comfortably. In the joy of that moment, Hislop gave herself a small pat on the back, but she knew this was the start of the story, not the end. If they were really going to change Australian politics, their methodology of co-operation and listening had to be further vindicated, and that meant seeing to it that Steggall, like Cathy McGowan before her, could repeat the win at the next election, as well as ensuring that more electorates availed themselves of the successful independents' model. And this is the wave that is continuing to roll through Australian electoral politics today.

Any attempt to understand the scale of the success Hislop and her team had must bear in mind some key points, not least of which is that these seats were never going to vote Labor or Greens, despite various demographic shifts and changes to electoral boundaries. What's more, in another era the candidates who ran as independents may well have been pre-selected by the Liberal Party itself, and much of the story of the independents' success in 2022 was about the way in which the party had made itself hostile territory for people like Hislop and Steggall, through a legacy of a suspicion towards women candidates in general, founded deep in the party's conservative and patriarchal past. Robert Menzies and the Institute of Public Affairs may have invited the Australian Women's National League (AWNL) to join as one of the original groups they assembled in the formation of the Liberal Party in 1944, but they only allowed the AWNL to have a role in party administration and fundraising, never as candidates. When, in the 1980s, party members Eve Mahlab and Julie Macphee formed the Liberal Feminist Network, they were shunned by a party trying to distance itself from the second-wave feminism it associated with the Whitlam government. In an article in the *Sydney Morning Herald,* author Julie Szego wrote that 'Unease with liberal feminism has solidified in the party's DNA to an extent I can't see any way of dislodging it without gender quotas. If the party is not forced to grapple with women's perspectives, it probably won't.'

The party's failure to recruit the likes of Steggall, Tink, Scamps, Ryan, Spender and Daniels was also a legacy of John Howard's purging of moderates (so-called 'wets') from the party ranks throughout his terms as prime minister, a process that continued – with a side-serving of Pentecostalism – under Scott Morrison. It was a process that eventually cost Malcolm Turnbull his job as party leader and prime minister, and Turnbull's fate was the eyes-wide-open moment for many of the Voices Of candidates.

In March 2022, on the #transitzone podcast (with which I was involved), Kylea Tink, who ended up winning the seat of North Sydney as an independent, said that she was 'very excited to see Malcolm Turnbull step up and become our prime minister because in him, I saw a whole heap of characteristics and values that I felt were speaking to me.' But, she added, she became disillusioned with how the party treated him. 'I suddenly saw that, whatever was going on at that federal level and within that party, that the voice of a forward-thinking statesman was just completely trampled on. And I just thought, wow, that's that. It is that environment pushing people like me out of the house.'

Incredibly, the under-threat Liberal candidates of

2022 all accused their independent opponents of being closet Labor or Greens candidates, or members of a secret party being controlled by Climate 200, the funding organisation founded by entrepreneur Simon Holmes à Court. They ran the line that Steggall and the others were 'fake' independents, one of the sillier and more tone-deaf responses employed by sitting candidates in contemporary politics, and it cost them dearly. It not only insulted the intelligence of their own voters, it reeked of desperation, and it spoke to the ways in which the Liberal Party had lost touch with its heartland voters. In another #transitzone interview, Peter Clarke and Margo Kingston asked Louise Hislop if she was ever worried about such accusations as deployed by the Liberal candidate in Mackellar, Jason Falinski, and her response tells us a lot about how the independents ended up winning.

Hislop said:

> we spend very little time thinking about him
> because this really isn't about him. This is about
> our community and how we want to be represented.
> He's just using that as narrative-making, that we
> are all centrally funded … which quite frankly is
> so insulting to all of us who have worked so hard
> to raise so much money within the community. So,
> actually, I mean, we're not concerned at all. But we
> do sometimes just have a little bit of a giggle and
> say we think he's panicking a little bit.

Hislop pointed out that Voices of Mackellar had 900-plus volunteers and noted that, 'if you've got 900 people, you can guarantee almost everyone in the electorate knows one of them. So, when [our opponents] call us fake independents, well, it's like, but that's my neighbour.' And this speaks to another important point: that the Voices Of movement was genuinely grassroots, part of their communities. From its initial success in Indi in 2013 to what happened in 2022, Voices Of movements began in local discussions, and it was from that process that candidates emerged. They didn't find a 'star' and try to drop them in and just tell people to vote for them. They organised community meetings and they let that process, and those involved in it, determine who would represent them. It was an approach that spoke to a level of trust in the good sense of the voters themselves, a trust that the Liberal Party leadership, particularly under Scott Morrison, had long since abandoned. Even Labor suffered a loss in their safe seat of Fowler in Western Sydney through the same neglect of local voices. They 'parachuted' in candidate and party heavyweight Kristina Keneally, only to see her lose to the conservative independent, and local, Dai Le.

In fact, while the Voices Of candidates were busy talking to their neighbours around kitchen tables, Scott Morrison was busy overriding the decisions of local Liberal Party pre-selection committees and imposing his own 'captain's picks' on electorates – a process that led to internal divisions of such magnitude that longstanding members initiated court cases against the party. As Morrison and his key supporter, Alex Hawke, were imposing candidates from on high, the Voices Of committees were letting them arise from the communities themselves.

And what candidates arose!

Zali Steggall, Sophie Scamps, Allegra Spender, Kylea Tink, Zoe Daniels and Monique Ryan were impressive women of incredible accomplishment, with everything from Olympic gold medals to a degree in paediatric neurology to their credit. Still, having a Zali Steggall as your candidate was one thing, but you also needed to tap into that zeitgeist, and through the values they espoused, the engagement they pursued, and the issues they championed, these independents did exactly that.

Scott Morrison's unlikely victory at the 2019 federal election lulled him, his party and the mainstream media into a false sense of security, and gave them a distorted view of what the zeitgeist was. For a while he seemed untouchable, but as the 2022 election approached, his thrusting superficiality, his lack of urgency when urgency was required, his apparent inability to empathise with anyone outside his own family, his increasingly public Pentecostalism, and his condescending attitude towards women left people deeply worried. They were concerned about a lack of effective action on climate change and what that would mean for their children. They were worried that too many important matters were simply being ignored or subsumed in pointless inter- and intra-party clashes that ignored the interests of voters themselves. There was a growing concern about integrity, from how taxpayers' money was being spent, to the honesty of the prime minister himself. In the successful 'teal' seats in particular – but really, throughout the country – people felt abandoned by business-as-usual, big party politics, and they wanted a more engaged, local representation.

At the 2022 federal election, not only did Steggall increase her majority, Louise Hislop and others used the same methodology – patient, painstaking, polite grassroots campaigning – in the neighbouring seat of Mackellar, and local doctor Sophie Scamps travelled the same route to victory. Hislop's childhood friend, photographer Leonie Scarlett, headed up Voices of Mackellar and set out along the same challenging path of engagement that Hislop had trod over the last several years. Scarlett has stressed the centrality of the kitchen table conversation approach, and has written:

> The model of the Kitchen Table Conversations
> brought together the affluent and the less affluent,
> the left and the right, men and women, old and
> young. They came from every suburb across
> this electorate and the messages came loud and
> clear. The political system is failing us, inclusion
> is a thing of the past, when did honesty and
> integrity become irrelevant, the system needs to be
> overhauled, fixed.

At Hislop's suggestions, Scarlett invited me to talk to her new group, and in the RSL Club in Newport, a stone's throw from where I was born, I spoke to another roomful of people keen to take control of their democratic lives. I had the same sense I'd had when I spoke to Voices of Warringah over a year earlier: that the Liberal Party were in for the fight of their life. Eventually, Dr Sophie Scamps, who was present that night but not yet installed as the candidate, would win the seat. Kylea Tink won in North Sydney using the same methodology. Cathy McGowan's successor in Indi, Helen Haines, was returned with an increased majority. Proving the resilience and power of the methodology, the Melbourne-based, Liberal blue-ribbon seats of Kooyong and Goldstein fell to Monique Ryan and Zoe Daniels respectively. Kate Chaney, the niece of Fred Chaney, a former Liberal Party 'wet' and deputy party leader in 1989, won the seat of Curtin in Western Australia as a Voices Of independent. Wentworth, which had gone to Dr Kerryn Phelps at the 2018 by-election, replacing Malcolm Turnbull, then returned to the Liberal Party at the 2019 federal election. It was won in 2022 by another independent, Allegra Spender. She was another disaffected Liberal with a long family history of party representation: her father was John Spender, a shadow minister under both Andrew Peacock and John Howard. Her grandfather was Sir Percy Spender, a cabinet minister under Robert Menzies, the founder of the Liberal Party.

There are many contemporaneous stories of organis-ations similar to Voices of Warringah and individuals like Louise Hislop around the country, including Denise Shrivell in North Sydney, who was involved with North

Sydney's Independent, as well as Reason Party candidate Jane Caro, who ran a Senate campaign. Shrivell is a powerhouse of online political activity, running a popular Twitter feed and a regular Friday live podcast (for which I have been interviewed), but she has put her skills to work in the 'real world' too. As she told me, 'For a long time now I've made the conscious decision to approach issues with tangible solutions, so my activities are about doing something to effect change as opposed to just talking (or tweeting) about change.'

It could well be the motto of the entire independents' movement.

In an excellent article in *The Monthly*, journalist Margaret Simons documented the rise of various independent candidates and shone a light on some of the regional examples, including Rob Priestly running in Nicholls; Pennie Scott, in Riverina; and teacher Penny Ackery, who was 'taking on Minister for Industry Angus Taylor in the sprawling NSW electorate of Hume'. One of the most incredible results happened in the electorate of Groom, in the rich agricultural area of Southern Queensland across the Darling Downs, a seat held by the terrifying margin of 20.5 per cent by Nationals MP Garth Hamilton. The independent challenger, Suzie Holt, didn't win, but she pulled off a swing of 13.4 per cent, moving the seat into the contestable category for the next election.

There seems little doubt that regional challenges by independents will be a growth area at the next election in the wake of the 2022 result. As Simons notes, many locals now see the National Party as the 'mining party' and feel they have mishandled important local issues like water management. She also notes that what is happening is better thought of as a 'foment' than the 'wave' it is usually described as, 'since it is a multiple bobbing up rather than a single, connected thing. There are different issues in each electorate, and a different ecosystem surrounding each candidate', and it is unlikely that this process will subside any time soon, especially now that there are so many examples of how powerful Crooks's methodology of kitchen table conversations, listening and local engagement can be.

One the key outcomes of this foment will be seen at the state level, as the Voices Of methodology is increasingly deployed at that level of government, and one of the major developments of these various campaigns is that there is now a professional infrastructure in place. Leading lights like Cathy McGowan and Denis Ginnivan regularly conduct Voices Of workshops around the country, with McGowan also running workshops on how to operate within parliament once you are elected. In addition, Anthony Reed, who helped get Phelps and Steggall elected, has established a communications agency, Populares, which has worked with Allegra Spender in Wentworth, Sophie Scamps in Mackellar, and Kylea Tink in North Sydney.

Another matter to note is the role played by Climate 200, the organisation founded by Simon Holmes à Court, which provided funding and advice for a number of the independent campaigns. Climate 200's role was,

I think, at times wildly exaggerated and often completely misunderstood, and the mainstream media consistently conflated the role of Climate 200 itself with the person of Holmes à Court, accusing him of being some sort of Svengali figure behind the scenes, deciding the teals' position on key policies, and thinking of Climate 200 as a political party in its own right. The accusations made by the media spoke to their inability to think beyond the box of traditional political practice. They had trouble accepting that such an organisation stood outside two-party, business-as-usual politics, and they failed to recognise the grassroots nature of the Voices Of movement. At an address to the National Press Club in February 2022, Holmes à Court was visibly bemused by the persistent questioning from the gallery, predicated on the idea that he was running a political party and not the incubator that Climate 200 was much closer to being. In an article in *The Saturday Paper*, Holmes à Court said that 'Climate 200 provided funding and expert advice, but always to boost and never as the bedrock.' He made an important point that put the role of Climate 200 into proper perspective, noting that if 'a community campaign can't assemble the social capital and wherewithal to attract hundreds of donations and volunteers, it's ultimately unlikely to secure the 30 000 or so votes required to win the seat.' Climate 200 could only have a role once this initial hurdle was crossed.

In pushing the Svengali angle, mainstream journalists may have blinded themselves to a more pertinent story: that, in fact, the Climate 200 relationship with the 'teals' was often rocky, and some Voices Of candidates – Suzie Holt in Groom, for instance – refused to accept Climate 200 money. During my research I heard concerns about the way in which Holmes à Court, through no fault of his own, became the face of the Voices Of movement, and his appearance at the Press Club was mentioned by several people as problematic. Holmes à Court himself quite rightly resisted mainstream media oversimplifications of his role, and he told the *7am Podcast* that 'Climate 200 is effectively a giving circle or a crowdfunding campaign. We had raised about twelve-and-a-half million dollars from 11 200 donors.' But, he said, they 'started off on Twitter', where they 'raised about $2 million', and this underlines the important role played by social media in all these campaigns, from the time of Cathy McGowan in Indi in 2013.

We need to take a moment and move ourselves outside the narrative that the media have tried to impose – and are still trying to impose – and realise what an extraordinary development the Voices Of movement represents in our politics. We need to recognise what a hit the Liberal Party has taken, and how their collapse reflects underlying changes in Australia's socioeconomic make-up – changes the Liberal Party had been ignoring for years, and that Scott Morrison was in active denial about. His Pentecostalism and the way he used church networks to repopulate the Liberal Party with preferred candidates proved to be particularly destructive. Census figures released after the 2022 election showed that for the first time ever, less than half the population identified as

Christian and that the biggest area of growth was among those who ticked the 'No religion' option. It underlined the extent of Morrison's miscalculation of the zeitgeist. Or his contemptuous dismissal of it.

Census data also shows that of the 15 electorates with the highest median income in the country, the Liberal Party now holds none of them. Zero. They used to hold 14 of the 20 wealthiest electorates in the country, and they now hold five. The party would need to win 18 seats to regain government at the next election, and analysis by David Tanner at *The Australian* suggested that if, as Peter Dutton and others have said, they were to concentrate on outer metropolitan seats rather than the 'teal' seats they lost in 2022, they are likely fighting a losing numbers game. Tanner notes, 'such a strategy would require the Coalition to win electorates on margins at least as high as 7.6 per cent, more than double the minimum required.' That is to say, the 18th most marginal seat in which they are a contender, Paterson, on the NSW mid-north coast, is on a margin of 3.3 per cent.

The same data shows that wealthy voters fled the Coalition; people with mortgages fled; people who rent and people whose children were educated in private schools also fled. People of Chinese heritage, in previous elections a reliable and growing part of the Coalition base, fled. The journey from Scott Morrison's 2019 'miracle' election win to the salted earth of the Coalition's 2022 electoral map is like something out of *Game of Thrones*, or perhaps *The Three Stooges*. The idea that Peter Dutton is the person to bring the party back to power and credibility, to reignite the zeitgeist in their favour, to reconnect with women, who are increasingly driving community politics, is delusional. The idea that Labor will be spared a similar reckoning is almost as fanciful, something the new government hasn't got its head around yet, as we shall see.

We also need to recognise that things could very easily have gone in a much less democratic direction, just as they have in other parts of the world. Australia has not been immune to various forms and intensities of right-wing populism, but the Voices Of movement has short-circuited a tendency on the rise since at least the appearance on the scene of Pauline Hanson and One Nation (and I note in passing that Hanson herself came close to losing her Senate seat). The previous centre-right formation of Australian political legitimacy – the Liberal Party – had moved into a more extreme right-wing position, with an increasing overlay of the sort of evangelicalism that has dominated the Republican Party in the United States, and it can no longer be said to hold that middle ground. We should be grateful that a band of pragmatic, local democrats moved in to fill that void and that they took as axiomatic that the grassroots were the key to their own success and their democratic legitimacy.

The Voices Of approach to local politics was not without its problems and faults, and later in the book I will spell out what I see as particular concerns. But its essential democratic character is something to be cherished. Not just cherished, but developed, so that the listening, co-operative approach that is at the heart of the methodology is extended as widely as possible, into all electorates and the institutions of the state.

We are witnessing other social, political and occupational transformations too, mainly at the hands of a technological revolution, of being a service economy rather than one based in manufacturing, with the whole idea of what constitutes a career changing beyond all recognition. The role of future parliaments will be to manage such changes, not just so that no-one is left behind, but so that people can live their best lives. If we really want that future to be democratic, progressive and egalitarian, we will need a politics that embodies those values in its day-to-day operation. The election of 21 May 2022 allowed us to see what was possible, and it was beyond what many of us would ever have dared to imagine. The challenge now is to make sure we don't slip back into the bad old ways of two-party dominance.

Part Two
How we got to 2022

*We are what we pretend to be, so we must
be careful about what we pretend to be.*

Kurt Vonnegut

2

Insiders and outsiders: The dispute at the heart of Australian politics

Power doesn't always corrupt.
Power always reveals.

Robert Caro

At the beginning of the 1980s, the two major political blocks that dominated Australian politics – the Labor Party and the Liberal–National Party Coalition (LNP) – decided that the Australian economy should be more open to the forces of world markets, and in that apparently simple idea we find the source of much of the turmoil that came to a head in the federal election of 2022. Under the influence of the Treasury Department (themselves under the influence of the intellectuals who had influenced the Thatcher and Reagan revolutions in Britain and the United States) first the Hawke–Keating government and then, after the 1996 election, the Howard government, transformed the Australian economy so that it would, in their rhetoric, become more competitive. These economic changes affected key aspects of our national identity and ushered in a period of great uncertainty about who were as a people, creating ongoing arguments about the sort of country we should be, and I think it is right to see the 2022 federal election as one of our most radical attempts to settle those arguments.

No culture is static, and most citizens don't expect it to stay the same forever, but they do want to hold onto some core idea of themselves. The idea of Australia that Prime Minister Scott Morrison was governing no longer lined up with the Australia that existed for most people, and the 2022 election was a reaction against what we sensed he and his government were turning us into. To put it slightly differently, the country had changed drastically over the previous 40 years, but there was an Australian essence that lingered and that most people wanted to hold onto, and it was that essence they felt Scott Morrison and the people around him were violating. Of course, ideas of 'national identity' are infinitely contested, and often fanciful, but none of this diminishes their power – if anything, it reinforces it – and it helps to look at a history of the ways in which politicians of all persuasions have used ideas of nation and belonging to consolidate their own power.

Politics can be brutally pragmatic, and ultimately governance depends on what policies are enacted and how. But politics is downstream from values, as has been said, and to understand something as disruptive as the election result of 21 May 2022, we need to have a sense of those values. So when I say 'Australia had changed',

I mean that we had made decisions about the way in which we were governed that were reflected in public policy, and this in turn had changed how we related to each other, perhaps not at a personal level, but certainly at the level of fellow citizens. The Voices Of movement was as successful as it was because it tapped into a discontent with national values that had been building over decades, and it is the origins of that discontent that we will look at here.

The Hawke–Keating government elected in March 1983 floated the dollar, deregulated the banking sector (allowing in foreign banks), removed tariffs, scaled back government support for various industries, and privatised everything from the Commonwealth Bank to Qantas. It also undermined (crushed) union power, flattened tax rates, and increased capital mobility, and all these changes acted in concert to increase inequality. The process also took power away from the national government and installed it in international instrumentalities such as the World Trade Organization, which added to people's sense that they had lost control over their national destiny (in many ways, they had). In those days, this set of policies was generally known as economic rationalism, but it is now more often called neoliberalism. The entire program was sold to the Australian people as not just necessary but overdue, in response to the alleged failures of Keynesian economics throughout the 1970s.

The LNP, in turn, supported all these changes and then, under John Howard, threw in a few of their own – privatising the job network, for instance. Just as significantly, the Howard government shifted hard right on social issues, setting up decades of what became known as the culture wars, and there was a direct correlation between the two: the more the new economic model undermined the material conditions for middle-class security – by, among other things, making jobs more precarious, making it more difficult to buy a home, and by concentrating wealth in the 1 per cent – the more stridently politicians like John Howard had to engage in a rhetoric of conservative normality.

Neoliberalism was obviously an economic pro-gram, but what is often overlooked is that it was backed with a moral imperative that exalted the role of the entrepreneurial individual, of so-called personal freedom, and it is here we find the real roots of the social transformation that was to reach its apotheosis in the person of Scott Morrison. Politics is downstream from values, and neoliberalism came complete with an underlying moral justification, and in many ways it is more accurate to see it as just that: a moral code, rather than an economic prescription. A connection between capitalism and morality was explicitly embedded in the neoliberalism of Milton Freidman and Friedrich von Hayek, the godfathers of our market society. Both made the link between market choice and moral choice and used it as a way of arguing against government involvement and regulation. 'The sphere where material circumstances force a choice upon us is the air in which alone moral sense grows and in which moral values are daily re-created in the free decision of the individual,' Hayek preached.

Doctrines like prosperity theology, which found expression in Scott Morrison's Pentecostalism, worked seamlessly with neoliberalism, allowing adherents to believe that there was something intrinsically moral in their own material success, that it represented tangible evidence of God's pleasure in what they were doing; and make no mistake, once a politician is convinced of the moral rightness of what he or she is doing, they will happily justify a lot of social disruption in the name of what they see as a greater good.

It would be foolish to say that there weren't benefits to the economic transformation Australia experienced, but the experiment has gone on long enough now that we are allowed to say that some of the hypotheses neoliberalism advanced have not come to fruition and that the social protections put in place have grown inadequate. By 2020, as pandemic swept the land, as assistance failed to materialise for many of those affected by flood and fire – sitting on the roofs of their houses as the floodwaters rose, or on beaches up and down the NSW South Coast as their homes burned – and as climate change threatened the viability of life on the planet, it became apparent to people that a society predicated on the hyper-individualism of neoliberalism was a really bad idea. That the freedom it offered was narrow and illusory. It became apparent that some things are not amenable to individual action, that they require a collective response, and by the time of the 2022 federal election we realised that we had severely diminished our ability to act collectively.

This became central to the motivations that inspired the Voices Of movement.

Australia was, at least, better situated than many countries. When they went down the neoliberal path, the Hawke–Keating government was still enough of a party of labour to put in place social protections against the market running free, not least of which was Medicare. In fact, when Greens leader Adam Bandt described the Hawke–Keating government as 'neoliberal' during an address to the Press Club after the 2022 election, Keating rejected the characterisation outright and called Bandt a 'bounder and a distorter of political truth'. The former prime minister's sensitivity to the neoliberal label is understandable, but there is an element of definitional hair-splitting in this. I think we can acknowledge the social protections Hawke–Keating put in place while still recognising the shift to a more market-based economy, with competition installed as a driver of policy. In the end, the die was cast, and there was something Shakespearean about what happened, with a party driven by a desire to improve the material and spiritual life of a nation embracing the tools of the enemy – free-market economics – succeeding beyond their wildest dreams but setting in train forces they could not control.

We became a less generous, less equal country.

We became less community-minded and more individualistic.

We lived less in a society and more in an economy.

None of this was entirely by design, but nor was it by accident. We changed the fundamental settings of the economy, turning everything from education to healthcare to unemployment benefits into opportunities for someone to make a profit and so, of course, people behaved differently. We privatised public services and replaced – certainly at the level of government – the moral imperative of care for our fellow citizens implicit in the idea of a welfare state with the incentives for profit of a market economy. Unemployment benefits, for example, became less about providing support to those without work and more about the unemployed 'earning' the right to this minimal payment through 'mutual obligations', strictures that remain in force – in some ways extended – under the Albanese government. We were less citizens and more customers, with even water and electricity and other life necessities in private hands, and this demanded a different mindset just to survive – a more individualistic, if not selfish self-understanding – and this new mindset crept in over the decades between the elections of 1983 and 2022. In the words of author Julianne Schultz, politicians became 'spruikers for the market and economics became the sole lingua franca of policy. The state was there to moderate and ensure the market flourished, rather than be the custodian of the public good.'

John Howard was expert at marrying the underlying moral presumptions of neoliberalism to a folksy story about families. He often told us that the best form of welfare was the family, thus justifying cuts to welfare – making it a personal responsibility rather than a state one – as well as helping to define the idea of worthy and unworthy recipients of government payments. Howard dressed his approach in the rhetoric of making us relaxed and comfortable with ourselves, and the theorists who helped sell his vision, particularly in the media, presented him as epitomising the sensible centre of Australian political life. But like a lot of self-styled centrists, the aim was less to do with compromise and balance than in normalising certain extreme beliefs. It was about redefining the right of the political spectrum as the centre.

Howard was part of a worldwide conservative tendency in the 1990s to marry radical liberal economics to social conservatism, a formula so racked with internal contradictions that it was bound to fail: how do you provide the material certainty on which social conservatism relies when you have made the economy vulnerable to unchecked market forces? One way is that you start blaming people themselves for the hardship your policies have manufactured, and Howard's prescriptions hardened into the rhetoric of the leaners and lifters of the Hockey–Abbott era, along with an increasingly conservative idea of family itself, and it is here we find the origins of LNP hostility to things like same-sex marriage, gender fluidity and, most especially, transsexualism, something that Scott Morrison leaned into heavily during the dying days of his government. Before we discuss the nature of Morrison's failure, though, let's dig a little more deeply into this idea of how we see ourselves and look at the way in which politicians deploy such ideas to their political advantage.

People of all nations tell stories about the sort of country they are, and what they leave out is as important as what they include. We accentuate the positive – someone once said that a nation is a place in which everyone has agreed to forget certain things. Despite this, stories of national identity are never uniformly positive, and so people constantly worry about where their country is heading, and about how they look to others. Indeed, social critics accentuate the *negative* in the hope of forcing people to do better: the failures of the past are held up as inspiration for a better future. At the time of the Mabo decision, for instance, then prime minister Paul Keating spoke on John Laws's radio program about our 'progress as a country truly at peace with itself inside'. It was a vision many Australians were not willing to recognise, and indeed, John Howard capitalised on such uncertainty throughout the term of his prime ministership. In fact, he stoked it.

My point is, the stories we tell ourselves about our nation affect our social wellbeing, the sort of place we want to be, and they are infinitely contested. In our short, post-colonisation history, certain words keep recurring when we have these discussions.

We are the lucky country.

We are practical.

We are ordinary.

We are sports-mad, masculine, the land of the fair go where egalitarianism rules.

Irreligious.

Irreverent.

Larrikins.

We are the most successful multicultural nation on earth.

The English may be polite, but Australians are friendly.

In more recent times, certain groups and people have pushed back against these characterisations, and much of our so-called culture wars are grounded in reactions to these concepts. For First Nations people, we are a colony. We are invaders. We are racist. For many others, Australia is anti-intellectual. Far from being the larrikin, anti-authoritarian children of convicts, we are the order-loving, police-friendly sons and daughters of their jailers.

To some degree, of course, we are all these things, while some of the more common descriptors – racist, patriarchal, sports-mad – are hardly unique to Australia. But within certain bounds, most Australians have a sense of themselves as radically equal, an idea that no-one is better than anyone else, that we are mates, that we look after each other, and that the government has a role in ensuring some level of equality is maintained. I think it is fair to say these are persistent strains in our national story, and that the Voices Of movement could not have succeeded without such a palette of values to draw from.

Has Australia ever been this egalitarian place of legend we comfort ourselves with?

Of course not.

As with every other Western democracy, our society is riven with division and disadvantage along lines of gender, ethnicity and class. Nonetheless, the mythology of our egalitarianism doesn't rest on nothing. Compared to Britain in particular, our most obvious point of contact, Australia has achieved a different settlement with notions of hierarchy that are, by any standard, more egalitarian than that of the 'mother country'. As historian John Rickard has put it:

> The unique and, to many, the perplexing achievement of Australian democracy has been to combine an egalitarian tradition with the politics of class. The contradiction is more apparent than real. Lacking a titled aristocracy and leisured class, colonial society encouraged an egalitarianism of manners. Such manners reflected not the absence of social stratification, but a means of coming to terms with it in a new setting.

I don't think I realised all this in a visceral way until I moved to London to live in 1991.

Having grown up with warm, familial feelings towards many things British, particularly its post-1950s music and its long literary tradition, I was completely shocked at the level of stratification within society – they even had second-class stamps! – and to discover the contempt in which most Australians were held. Particularly among the upper classes, Australia was seen as little more than a colony of uncultured slobs, our egalitarianism interpreted, literally, as a lack of *class*. What made it worse – if not laughable – was that I had arrived there in the early 1990s and Britain itself was flailing, still trying to make sense of itself post-Thatcher, with all the 'Little Englander' prejudices that would tear the country apart during Brexit and the subsequent demise of Boris Johnson already apparent, the glaring empire-shaped hole (as Salman Rushdie described it) at the heart of national identity, and outdated attitudes to gender, sexuality and race that they dared to accuse Australia of being uniquely guilty of.

The image of Australia that persisted in Britain was one set in aspic from the 1950s, and there is nothing like a dose of condescension from people who think they're better than you to activate your patriotic glands and get the hometown juices flowing. I suddenly found myself thinking about my country in a completely different way. I returned home in 1995, just before the election that removed Paul Keating and installed John Howard, and already it was apparent that the neoliberalism unleashed by the Labor government, and which would be nurtured by the Coalition government, was influencing the national mindset. The inequality baked into neoliberalism was manifesting as a national debate framed in terms of ordinary Australians versus elites, and I will say more about that below. What was most obvious was that the idea of Australian citizenship was a hot topic. Federal governments (Labor and non-Labor) had launched reports into the state of Australian citizenship over the previous 20 years, and one of the key political issues of the day was whether Australia should become a republic.

To understand how we got to the changes wrought by the 2022 election, it is useful to have a sense of the history of Australian citizenship, so let's dig into that a little more.

Most discussion begins with the recognition of the fact that the Australian Constitution does not mention either citizenship or citizens. Nor is there a formal bill of rights. The British character of membership of the Australian state is central. Political scientist Alastair Davidson points out that from 'its first formal statement of what it is to be a citizen in Australia, the Australian state has made it clear that its primary concern was to establish in a country of immigration that the newcomers show clearly that they have adopted the national identity, that they have joined the national family of British descent.'

The peak manifestation of this was the *Immigration Restriction Act* of 1901, popularly (and accurately) known as the White Australia Policy, which was the first major legislation passed by the newly federated government. 'Whiteness' defined not only a sense of Australian identity but was also a formal requirement of membership of the state. Subsequent 'naturalisation acts' reinforced the notion, and as debate on a 1903 amendment to the Act makes clear, the intention was to exclude anyone not white and European. Queensland senator Henry Bournes Higgins said in parliamentary debate:

> The object of this amendment is to prevent
> any of the 80 000 coloured aliens who are not

naturalized at present ... from applying for
Commonwealth naturalization papers ... I
wish to make a distinction between them and
immigrants who come from Germany, Italy, and
other countries in Europe. As regards [the] idea
that this Bill should admit persons from all parts
of the earth to the same rights and privileges
which we possess, I have not yet reached that
stage of magnanimity.

But such exclusions tended to hide more positive aspects
of Australian approaches to citizenship. Under the
influence of political movements such as the Levellers,
the Chartists and utilitarianism, Australia pioneered
parliamentary and democratic reforms that enhanced
the practical meaning of democratic citizenship – even
as we lacked a formal definition of it – and pushed us in a
direction far more egalitarian than the British homeland.
These included universal suffrage by 1904; the secret
ballot, which for a number of years around the world
was known as the Australian ballot; the equalisation
of territorial constituencies to overcome problems with
gerrymandering; the abolition of plural voting, whereby
university graduates and business proprietors could
vote more than once; and the payment of members of
parliament (introduced at a state level in the 1880s),
which meant that it wasn't just the wealthy who could
run for parliament.

You can see the roots of the Voices Of movement in
such innovations.

Alfred Deakin, who would become our second prime minister in 1903, expressed the prevailing attitude among the founders when he said:

The best thing that Australians could do was to make the country so productive, so good a place to live, and bring about such just and fair conditions, with such fair opportunities for earning an honest living, such protection against monopolies, with such fair chances for all men who were prepared to go on the land and work for industries, that other people would also want to become Australians.

Of course, this fairness did not extend to people of other races, and not to women, and the situation of the First Nations population clearly showed the way in which citizenship embodied notions of exclusion and violence. The formal political process of exclusion, overriding Indigenous sovereignty, was marked by several key legislative events, beginning with the Constitution itself, but more importantly with a range of federal and state legislation that sought to control and regulate the Indigenous population. Historians John Chesterman and Brian Galligan write that First Nations' people were only mentioned twice in the Constitution, and in both cases 'by way of exclusion – from the section 51(26) race power and the section 127 census count'.

That this is a history of racism, discrimination and exclusion there can be no doubt, and it is important to note that claims to sovereignty, rights and recognition by and for First Nations peoples have existed since long before the country was first occupied as a British penal colony in 1788, and that such recognition is central to any understanding of Australian citizenship more generally. Even with their formal recognition as citizens, with the creation of the category 'Australian Citizen' via the 1948 *Commonwealth Citizenship Act*, few if any benefits of membership flowed to First Nations people. More positive developments – including the 1967 referendum ceding jurisdiction of Aboriginal and Torres Strait Islander issues to the federal government, the Mabo and Wik High Court decisions of the 1990s which recognised the concept of native title, the instigation of a formal process of reconciliation, and the National Apology by the Rudd government – have been much more recent. The new Albanese government has made constitutional recognition of First Nations people central to its first term of government, and, as we shall see, the role of the new crossbench will be important to the success of that process.

Australian citizenship, then, was constructed within a framework of British subjecthood rather than any distinctive Australian identity. It was predicated on major exclusions, specifically 'non-white' people, including those indigenous to the Australian landmass itself, and it was not supported by a formal recognition of rights. As well, the patriarchal nature of society diminished the standing of women, undermining their role as citizens. Our citizenship nonetheless reflected an egalitarian approach to class, with innovations such as the secret ballot and MP salaries allowing the inclusion of the working class as members of parliament. It represented a unique settlement, the nature of which was not seriously challenged until after World War II. To quote Galligan and Chesterman again:

> Australian citizenship has been defined and developed through legislation, administrative practice and public policy by both Commonwealth and State governments in key political, civil, social and economic areas. There was no historical moment or place of articulation, nor is there a core definition of citizenship or statement of citizens' rights and duties.

Although values such as equality and egalitarianism are often more honoured in the breach than the practice, their articulation is important because it forces us, over time, to deal with the contradictions between stated values and practice. By the end of the 1960s, this ongoing development included the abolition of the White Australia policy, an increasingly bipartisan policy of multiculturalism, and the growth throughout the 1970s, 1980s and 1990s of an intensifying debate about Australia formally becoming a republic. These changes were never uniform nor entirely predictable, and they could throw up complications that made general statements of identity problematic: a patrician conservative like Malcolm Fraser was more progressive on Asian immigration, for instance, than he was about the possibility of a Labor government.

Indeed, the move to a pluralist conception of citizenship and national identity was led by educated elites more comfortable with the cosmopolitanism implied by these policies, and who had the institutional power with which to facilitate such a shift. This was accompanied by a tendency – far from universal but nonetheless perceptible – to disparage aspects of a more traditional, white Australian identity and see it, one-dimensionally, as racist, sexist and anti-intellectual.

Commentaries on the sterility, parochial nature and anti-intellectualism of the 'ordinary Australian', particularly the 'suburban Australian', were common among commentators and intellectuals. Academic Alan Gilbert wrote in an essay about suburbia that 'Divided on almost everything else, the "left" and "right" of the intellectual spectrum agreed on this one thing at least. They hated suburbia. They despised it.' Poet A.D. Hope wrote in his poem *Australia* of 'five cities, like five teeming sores', and that 'The river of her immense stupidity // Floods her monotonous tribes from Cairns to Perth', and it pretty much catches the contempt many intellectuals felt for their homeland. The perception among those often called 'ordinary Australians' that they were being demonised in this way generated a backlash, unsurprisingly, and its own forms of exaggeration, and perhaps even a tendency to reject ideas such as multiculturalism and republicanism simply because they were seen to be associated with 'elite opinion'.

And this raises another key aspect of Australian identity that came to a head in the period of the Morrison government. Traditionally, Australians have maintained a relatively positive, if nonetheless antagonistic, working relationship between citizen and state, embodied in the reforms mentioned earlier (such as the secret ballot and universal suffrage). We have understood ourselves to be involved in a social experiment, one that was largely democratic in nature, though it embodied 'exclusions', particularly those associated with race. This experiment coalesced around the time of federation in what journalist Paul Kelly has called the Australian Settlement. Kelly writes:

> Australia was founded on: faith in government authority; belief in egalitarianism; a method of judicial determination in centralised wage-fixing; protection of its industry and its jobs; dependence upon a great power … for its security and finance; and, above all, hostility to its geographical location, exhibited in fear of external domination and internal contamination from the peoples of the Asia/Pacific.

This positive relationship between citizens and the state stands in stark contrast to the relationship that prevailed (prevails) in the United States, though the advent of neoliberalism, and its focus on the individual at the expense of the collective, has brought with it an upswing in Australia of the American-style hostility to government. We saw these attitudes accentuated during the pandemic, with loose coalitions of fringe conspiracy theorists united around the idea of what they insisted was a 'freedom' agenda. They marched in the streets, despite – or because of – the existence of official lockdowns, insisting on their right to ignore public health measures. For these groups, freedom was defined as freedom *from* government interference rather than more expansively as the freedom *to* live the life you wanted, the latter a conception that relied less on individual rights and more on collective responsibility to other citizens. Your right to swing your arm ends at the tip of my nose, as the saying goes. That is to say, the issue was not whether the directive to wear a mask on public transport during a pandemic infringed your individual rights – it obviously did – but whether your right to breathe germs on everyone else should trump their right not to catch Covid.

The freedom marchers – 'cookers', as they were sometime called – didn't see it that way, and although their philosophy held little sway during the 2022 election, it had nonetheless infiltrated civil society in a way that it hadn't previously and that had been enabled by the overall economic morality of neoliberalism itself. Still, Australia's history of national identity had different roots to that of the Americans such protesters communicated with online. As constitutional scholar Harley Wright has put it:

> In contrast to post-revolutionary Americans, who regarded government as 'inherently dangerous', Australians had a far more trusting attitude towards government … the emphasis was not so much upon the need to 'distribute and separate

mistrusted governmental power' but rather to make it [government] a more effective instrument of the popular will.

In the US, the tension between state and citizen is often manifested in martial terms, and the Second Amendment of the US Constitution, which allows the existence of armed militia, is a particular protection against a rogue state. But in Australia, John Howard was able to tap into a different tradition when, in the wake of the Port Arthur massacre, he instigated a gun buyback program and enacted stronger laws around ownership of firearms. This willingness to see the relationship between government and citizens in a more benign, less antagonistic light – one that didn't require armed militias as its legitimating guarantee – is central to Australian ideas of national identity.

This means that in Australia disputes between the people and the government tend to manifest in a more class-based manner and are often presented as a conflict between elites and the ordinary people. The 2022 election, and the changes it wrought to our political system, were part of an organic response to this sort of dispute, and I will spell that out in more detail as the book progresses. For now, let's concentrate on how this sort of disputation has been understood, particularly in the time since the Howard government, because I think that is the central moment.

When I returned from living in London in 1995, the idea of an elite–popular divide was the defining issue of Australian politics. Not only was John Howard milking it for all he was worth – presenting himself as the champion of 'ordinary Australians' – intellectuals and activists within the Labor Party were also arguing strongly that the party had lost touch with its working-class roots and was in thrall to what were characterised as 'inner-city elites', among other disparaging labels. The elder Kim Beazley, a minister in the Whitlam government, had famously said that within the party 'the cream of the working class' had been replaced by 'the scum of the middle class'.

Robert Manne, the dominant public intellectual of the period, wrote in 1998 that 'Australian party politics is … currently overshadowed by a single, central problem: how to bridge the chasm, in interest and sentiment, that has opened between what I call, for want of better terminology, the ordinary people and the elites.' The characterisation still has resonance, and in the wake of the 2022 election, the new Liberal leader, Peter Dutton, instantly fell back on a version of it. He concocted a Frankenstein's monster that tried to stitch together Howard's contempt for 'elites' with Robert Menzies's delineation of a new middle class, those he called 'the forgotten people'. Dutton's ploy was an anachronistic, gothic approach and it will fail for reasons I spell out at the end of the book, but let's not underestimate how powerful this characterisation of Australian society can be.

Under the influence of neoliberalism, precedence was given to the idea of a market that found its own equilibrium among the unconstrained actions of individuals, rather than to the idea of a society that managed itself in the interests of the common good. As such, we allowed a situation to develop whereby many political decisions were seen as flawed because they were made within institutions suffering from what theorist John Uhr called a deliberative deficit. 'Too many decisions are made,' he wrote, 'by too few people in too little time on the basis of too little information', and it was this growing sense that we were losing control over our own destiny that ignited the pushback we saw in the form of the Voices Of movement, and the Purple Sage discussion groups that preceded it.

In Manne's conception of an elite–popular divide, it was the ordinary Australians who felt ostracised, left out of the decision-making processes as a neoliberal elite imposed technocratic solutions upon every economic and social problem that arose. There was a lot of truth to this, but characterisations such as 'elite–popular divide' were fraught. Theorist McKenzie Wark argued that 'whenever anyone tries to draw a line through Australian culture, whether it be mateship/meritocracy or skip/wog or Melbourne/Sydney or Ascendancy/vernacular or whatever, we are dealing with a fantasy.' Wark's caution is worthwhile, but such line-drawing is more an oversimplification than an out-and-out fantasy. The elite–popular divide had a basis in reality. It dominated comment on the Republican referendum, the Pauline Hanson phenomenon, and electoral politics in general. Its use was widespread among commentators, journalists, academics and politicians and became central to the analysis of matters of politics and culture in Australia. Former federal health minister Carmen Lawrence, in an address to the Sydney Institute in August 2000, said:

> Many Australians I talk to are disgruntled by a system which does not appear to respond to their needs and seems, increasingly, to be in the hands of elites more interested in their own advancement than the general good. As a result, our political system has less and less legitimacy.

Academic Katharine Betts referred to the so-called 'great divide', saying that 'Since the 1960s many members of the new class had begun to construct a liberal cosmopolitan identity for themselves, an identity which was built upon emphasising their distance from the selfishness and racism which they attributed to parochial Australians.' Another academic, Greg Melleuish, wrote of a divide between 'a new cosmopolitan elite and a democratic mass'. A more polemical, if not satirical, characterisation was offered by journalist Imre Salusinszky. He spoke of what he called the 'Wetworld', which he defined as 'a nation-within-a-nation that boasts its own religion (the Uniting Church), its own political party (the Democrats), its own think-tank (ACOSS), even its own national broadcasting network (the ABC) … Above all, Wetworld has provided a secure platform from which artists and intellectuals have been able to maintain their long campaign against the economic and social arrangements that underwrite their own prosperity and freedom of expression.'

The most contentious adoption of the language of an elite–popular divide belonged to writings associated with the One Nation Party. Their website gave considerable space to right-wing politicians and writers, and in one section, written by former Labor politician Graeme Campbell and political commentator Mark Uhlmann, they argued that:

> Australian Leadership elites in politics, the bureaucracy, academia, big business, the churches and the media have effectively cut themselves adrift from the interests of the majority of Australians. Many have betrayed the trust of the people they are supposed to represent … As part of this process the elites, while they may mouth concern for the country, have given up thinking in terms of the national interest to pursue an internationalist agenda. This agenda is eroding the foundations of our nation and marginalising the majority, which has less and less say in its destiny … The bulk of the media, charged with a watchdog role in the public interest, have become active agents in this process. Academics, artists and others who are supposed to be independent-minded have become propagandists and intellectually corrupt hirelings.

From the other end of the political spectrum, Indigenous leader Noel Pearson, in his Light on the Hill speech, identified an elite–popular divide as being a contemporary way of talking about class itself. According to Pearson, we had '[abandoned] class in our intellectual analysis of our society and history'. He said that 'classes are treated as political constituencies and labelled with evocative and provocative terms such as "the battlers" and "the mainstream" and "the forgotten people" and "the elites".' Writer and theorist Michael Thompson suggested a similar class analysis in his diagnosis of the Labor Party, writing that 'the takeover of the ALP in the wake of the Whitlam era by the tertiary educated (with their contempt for the contribution to Labor of the under-educated) [caused] the post-war exodus of the working class from the ALP's branches', and he echoed the words of Betts and Melleuish in suggesting the party had been captured by 'special interest groups who conned Labor governments into imposing their own agendas on ordinary Australians'.

Discussion of an elite–popular divide, as well as being linked to issues of class, was also linked to issues of identity and security, and one way of understanding its resonance was as a way for various elites to understand themselves and their relationship to their societies. It represented a response to 'the changing nature of political events and ideology in a post-industrial society', something that former Labor leader – and now member of One Nation – Mark Latham argued in his book *Civilising Global Capital*. It was, he suggested, an attempt to replace the dichotomy of capital versus labour that dominated post-war politics with a framework that better reflected neoliberal developments such as the 'enhanced mobility of capital, the emergence of an information society, changes in work, and the transformation of social institutions [that] have fractured the effectiveness of the old ideological divide'.

All these issues emerged again as we drew closer to the 2022 election, but they emerged in a world fundamentally different from that of the 1980s and 1990s.

There is no doubt that the concept of an elite–popular divide can be used to force debate in a particular direction, to evade more important questions, and to slice concepts in a way favourable to one set of players or another. It draws on an implicit understanding that in a democracy, the legitimacy of any action derives from the support given to it by a majority of the citizens. Thus, to suggest that any given position has 'popular support' is to imbue it with democratic legitimacy. On the other hand, to be able to label something as the wishes of an 'elite' – by definition and popular understanding, a minority of the population – is to undermine its legitimacy. There was, therefore, a strong sense in which the rhetoric of an elite–popular divide was (and is) a way for one side in various arguments to marshal a majority opinion that they could then claim to be following. The term 'elite' deployed in this way hid the fact that those using it were themselves elites, and we need to recognise this rhetorical deception.

In the republican debate of the late 1990s, for instance, opinion polls consistently showed most Australians to be in favour of becoming a republic. However, the model on offer in the 1999 referendum to facilitate this constitutional change involved the appointment of the president by the parliament. The alternative model of direct, popular election had been controversially rejected by a Constitutional Convention. Opponents of the move to a republic were therefore able to characterise the appointment model as 'elitist' and sought to associate its implementation with perhaps the most unpopular elite within the country: federal politicians. They were able to present the alternative model, direct popular election of the president – which was not on offer – as the 'genuinely' democratic alternative, the model that had been rejected by the Convention, with the event itself characterised as a 'gabfest' among elites.

The monarchist side of the argument consistently invoked the notion of an elite–popular divide in the run-up to the republican referendum, and used as their campaign slogan 'Say no to the politicians' republic'. Although they were advancing perhaps the most 'elite' alternative – *monarchy*, for heaven's sake – and counted among their membership federal politicians they dismissed elsewhere as 'elite', they were able to position the 'No' vote as the status quo, the system that had 'served us well for a hundred years'. They were able to characterise the appointed president model as the tool of elites foisting their version of a republic on an unwilling country. In other words, they won support for retaining the monarchy by making a 'Yes' vote appear to be an elitist position – quite the bait and switch.

All these notions of identity and citizenship

connected to the changing economic organisation of the country under the relentless pressure of neoliberalism. Academic Cathy Greenfield suggested that:

> Since the ascendance [sic] of John Howard to leader of the Coalition parties … an ideological rhetoric dividing the social into differences between so-called 'elites' and so-called 'battlers' … has gained widespread cultural and media currency … In turn, this is a recrudescence of Australian liberalism's notions of national character and national identity, of 'national traditions' and 'national spirit' … is a recrudescence updated with neo-liberal inflections, and … [w]ith the neo-liberal colonization of the category of 'battlers' [and] what is increasingly asserted is a 'globalized' notion of human nature in the figure of the rational autonomous individual who may be 'doing it hard' but can calculate just where his or her (private) interests lie. These are the individuals who constitute a shareholding democracy.

These matters were sources of conflict in society and, as such, could be mobilised by political players. But we always have a choice in how we deal with this sort of conflict, and what is extraordinary about the 2022 election is that ordinary citizens – via grassroots organisations – took back from the professional politicians the power to define the nature of this conflict, and in the process redefined the essential nature of the elite–popular divide itself. We moved beyond it and towards a bottom-up redefinition of the divisions within society, and what emerged was the voice of a nascent knowledge class that didn't necessarily fit traditional class structures; one that reflected not just the changing nature of work, but the growing role of women within the traditional working class.

Most importantly, this new force chose to view the conflict arising less as a clash between ordinary people and the elites and more as an opportunity for deliberation among people they considered equal, but not all of whom had access to the levers of political power. And at that point, the elite–popular divide transformed into an argument between insiders and outsiders, between a political class and the vast bulk of people not directly involved in politics. With amazing speed and success, beginning in the rural Victorian seat of Indi in 2013, then extending to electorates all over the country in the run-up to the 2022 election, the non-political class developed grassroots workarounds – kitchen table meetings, public talks and gatherings and the like, and, most importantly, social media – that usurped the power of the traditional parties and other sources of power within the country, including the legacy media, and put the election of 2022 on a much more democratic footing than we had become used to seeing.

The change we witnessed on 21 May 2022 was not one that overthrew established sources of power in Australia and the automatic stabilisers that kept them in place – they are all still there – but it was one that gracefully stepped around them, or ignored them, revealing a certain hollowness in their construction, none more so than in the two-party system itself.

Central to all this was that ill-defined but powerful notion of Australian citizenship. When I was invited to speak with the various Voices Of groups, we discussed the idea of citizenship, and I argued that they had more in common with a version derived from the Greek city-state. I argued that democracy is self-rule, not rule by political parties, something I thought Voices Of organisations, based around finding independent candidates, needed to hear. Parties are not mentioned in the constitutions of any major democracy: not in ours, the American, the French, or the Canadian. Parties can be useful, and they can help organise our politics, which is inherently messy, particularly the legislative branch of government, and they can bring some unity and simplification to the complexity of governance. But they can also bring stasis, an inertia that makes it hard to get things done.

The French philosopher Simone Weil wrote a treatise against political parties in the wake of World War II, saying, 'If one were to entrust the organisation of public life to the devil, you could not invent a cleverer device' than the political party. Vida Goldstein would concur. Both women were concerned that the loyalty of members was to the party and not to the citizens they purportedly represented, and this was exactly the problem the Voices Of people were being confronted with, and which they were trying to solve. When parties dominate, our democracy stops being a participative one and becomes a representative one. Once you have parties involved in politics, once you move away from self-rule to representative rule, you end up with a lot of other intervening structures between citizens and government. Under such circumstances, parties can be captured by special interests, by donors, by other people of influence, and that necessarily means local voices are excluded. It can also lead to corruption. If parties don't guard against all this, they risk becoming the opposite of what they should be, not a broad church but a narrow faction. They risk becoming 'captured' by external players. This doesn't happen on every issue, but it can happen on key issues like climate change. And this means that you can have the best, most enlightened local member when it comes to climate change, but at the end of the day, because they are a member of a party, they will have to vote the way the party wants them to vote.

Party identity overrides national identity, and citizens are left behind.

Sound familiar?

I had been told by many of those I spoke with in Mackellar that they had no problem with their local Liberal representative, Jason Falinski, and many of them spoke of him as a pretty good bloke. He seemed, personally, to want to do more about climate change, which had already emerged as the key issue for the Voices Of organisations. But I pointed out that when push came to shove, Jason Falinski was going to vote the same way as Barnaby Joyce.

This was precisely the revelation that was already

dawning on those present, and this line of argument went on to be central – and powerful – in the rhetorical dillybag of the 'teal' independents. Party unity, party discipline, the practice of which had been the hard carapace protecting generations of male politicians, was about to flip over and expose its soft underbelly. The idea that politics required a party structure at all was being called into question, and the rigidity of political hierarchy was being recognised as an impediment to good public policy, rather than an enabler of it. All that was solid was melting into air, and Australian politics could no longer be represented on a straight line, only on a soft grid.

Until the advent of neoliberalism in the early 1980s, Australian politics had been dominated by a constant fight between the conservative right of the country, represented by the Liberal–National Party Coalition and its earlier iterations, and the working-class left of the country, represented by the Labor Party. To call this a two-party system was a bit of a fudge even then, given that one of its main components, the Coalition, itself consisted of two parties, the metropolitan-based Liberal Party and the rural-based National Party (and, later, the amalgamated LNP in Queensland). But the truth is, most people thought of the LNP as a single entity, and in many key respects it was, and certainly the media presented it as such. In the immediate aftermath of World War II, the arguments between the two major parties cleaved strongly to international divisions between left and right, between socialism and free-market economics, but by the time of the Hawke–Keating government, these categorisations were collapsing. Once the Labor Party went all-in on neoliberal economics, the old class divisions started to lose their power, and our sense of personal and national identity shifted with it.

Until then, the combination of clear party identification, and an electoral system that required everyone to vote, created a sense of cohesion and stability about our politics. Compulsory voting meant politicians couldn't isolate and ignore certain segments of society in the way that happened in America. Preferential voting allowed enough flexibility into the system that other choices were possible, but the flow of preferences was always towards the two major parties, and that, too, created a sense of stability. It also created a secure status quo.

After 1996, from the period of the Howard government, the nation's identification with these 'two' parties started to shift and then fade away. Opinion polls consistently showed that both the LNP and Labor each struggled to gain more than 30 per cent of the primary vote, and indeed, the result of the 2022 election bore these figures out. The Liberals (with the Nationals) ended up with a 35.8 per cent primary, while Labor had 32.6 per cent, one of the smallest primary votes by a party forming government in the nation's history.

In the Senate, thanks to a system of proportional representation, a certain diversity of representation had already installed itself, overwhelming two-party dominance, and, except for the final term of the Howard government (2004–07), the Senate could be relied upon to give neither of the major parties a clear majority. It was clear that people liked this check on the power of the lower house; that they saw the Senate as less a states' house than a house of review, and that this experience had undermined the strength of traditional arguments about the need for two-party 'stability' in the House of Representatives.

From 1996 onwards, first preference votes started shifting to smaller parties and independents in increasing numbers. The Greens, the Democrats, One Nation, and Centre Alliance, along with various independents, picked up an increased number of first preference votes between them, even if those votes didn't necessarily translate into seats in the house. Independents Ted Mack, Phil Cleary, Peter Andren, Graeme Campbell, Paul Filing, Pauline Hanson, Alan Rocher, Bob Katter, Tony Windsor, Rob Oakeshott, Andrew Wilkie, Cathy McGowan and Kerryn Phelps have held seats in federal parliament, culminating in the 15-member crossbench elected in 2022. On one reading, this trend is pulling apart the settlement that had provided security and certainty since 1945; but on another, it represents the country working towards a new settlement, a new solution to the ongoing problem of political representation.

The fact is, our parliament was failing to properly look like the diverse place the country was. It was at odds with the increasingly socially progressive place the country had become. So whereas less than 1 per cent of Australians worked as political consultants or lobbyists, such operatives made up a disproportionate 11.9 per cent of parliament. Party and union administrators were also a vanishingly small part of the general population (again, less than 1 per cent) but they made up 8.4 per cent of parliament. On the other hand, nurses made up 2.1 per cent of working Australians (there are 220 000 of them), but there was precisely one former nurse in parliament. Tradespeople were 13.5 per cent and teachers 3.5 per cent of the general population, but each constituted just 0.4 per cent of parliament.

In terms of ethnicity and gender, it was even more marked: 6 per cent of parliamentarians came from non-English-speaking backgrounds, compared to 23 per cent for the rest of us. Women may have held up half the sky, but they made up just 29 per cent of the House of Representatives and 39 per cent of the Senate. Labor was 44 per cent women to 56 per cent men – a good result achieved with a quota system – while the Coalition ran at an embarrassing 20 per cent to 80 per cent.

By the time Labor under Kevin Rudd wrested government back from the LNP in 2007, after 11 years of the Howard government, the old verities of party stability no longer held, though perhaps it wasn't immediately apparent. In fact, the first sign that something was amiss – in the sense that what we were dealing with was not business as usual – emerged in the leadership of the two major parties, when we saw both the Liberals and Labor changing leaders at an unprecedented and once unthinkable rate. This leadership instability reflected an underlying crisis of identity within the major parties themselves as they struggled to define the precise constituency they represented. Issues around the changing nature of work meant that the idea of a working class had changed drastically, thus undermining Labor's traditional relationship with that core constituency. The Liberal–National Party Coalition, traditionally the parties of metropolitan and rural capital respectively, increasingly found themselves at loggerheads with new centres of capital, such as the tech industry, and were drawn into culture-war type alliances with people who would once have been seen as Labor's core vote. The Coalition's traditional role was purely and simply to oppose organised labour, but with the collapse of unionism, and the growing shift in the working experience of most Australians, this alone was no longer the basis for a firm party identity.

In hindsight, we can say that one clear sign of what was in store was the success of the equal marriage plebiscite in November 2017, which delivered a resounding 'Yes' vote, particularly in the Liberal electorates that fell in 2022 to the independents, but across the country as well. That result destroyed the ability of far-right conservative groups like the Australian Christian Lobby, or even the Liberal Party itself, to pretend that their views of family and marriage were supported by 'quiet Australians' or the 'silent majority'. It opened a space on the new grid of Australian politics for the fiscally conservative, socially progressive 'teals' to claim as their own.

By the time of the 2022 election, the elite–popular divide had morphed. More and more, it was the educated elite who felt ostracised from a political class that they saw as failing in their basic job of governance. Climate change was central, not just threatening the life chances of the next generation, but illustrative of the way in which mainly the Liberal Party, but also Labor, were failing to heed expert advice. This tendency was reinforced during the early stages of the Covid pandemic too, where the advice of health experts, let alone those capable of producing a vaccine, had become an immediate matter of life and death.

Environmentalists had long been ostracised by governments of both major Australian parties, who ignored clear scientific evidence and advice and continued to enact policies – particularly around energy – as if business-as-usual extraction and energy generation, with a few tweaks here and there, could slow down the process likely to make life on large swathes of the planet – many of them in Australia – unliveable. The Liberal–National Party was ruled by climate-change denialists who vetoed every attempt by the more moderate (saner) members of the Coalition to enact policies that took climate change seriously. They were in thrall to mining and energy companies and captured more by *their* interests than the interests of the citizens themselves.

The whole country was being held hostage to a tiny, anti-science faction within the ruling parties (Labor had theirs too) that was turning the country into an international climate pariah, if not ground zero for the increasingly severe effects of climate change itself.

The key point of cleavage, then, was no longer between ordinary people and elites, as it had been spoken of from the 1990s onwards, but between insiders and outsiders. The insiders were the political class – including the media – who had become a self-reinforcing, self-referential group who mainly spoke to and for themselves. They gave each other jobs, positions on boards, and roles in government agencies. A post-election report by the Grattan Institute showed that a 'significant and growing percentage of appointees have political connections to the government that appointed them', and that across 'all federal government appointees, 7 per cent have a direct political connection. This figure rises to 21 per cent among those positions that are well paid, prestigious, and/or powerful. For the Administrative Appeals Tribunal (AAT), an important body that makes rulings on government decisions, the figure is 22 per cent', thanks to appointments by the Morrison government. They interviewed each other in newspapers (or their electronic equivalents) and on radio and television shows, one of which was literally called *Insiders*.

Meanwhile, under Scott Morrison, the Liberal Party was becoming increasingly Pentecostal, with the prime minister intervening in the party's pre-selection processes on behalf of his preferred candidates. Internal party factions destroyed Malcolm Turnbull's prime ministership, which was the last straw for many of those who ended up in the Voices Of movements, the point at which lifelong Liberals realised that the party had left them and so it was time for them to leave the party. As Cathy McGowan told journalist Margo Kingston, 'The Liberal Party has swung right and has swung conservative Christian'. She said she asked people in cosmopolitan, metropolitan seats, 'It's only going to get worse, so how are you going to vote?'

It is no coincidence, given all this, that not only did the independents movement arise within the most well-to-do and highly educated electorates in the country, but that they found as their key issue climate change itself. A combination of young people newly activated by a lack of action on climate change, and a class of knowledge workers – a term recently resurrected by journalist Guy Rundle – whose material needs were being ignored, could see that much of the political class had been captured by denialists and conspiracy theorists like George Christensen and Craig Kelly, with Pauline Hanson and her band of quasi-racists and anti-science fruitcakes cheering from the sidelines and on *Sky After Dark*.

In saying all this, I am not arguing for a return of the technocracy, a rule by experts, or any other narrow conception of governance that was reflected in the so-called elite–popular divide of the 1990s. I *am* saying that a lot of the anti-science people, the conspiracy theorists and the rest of them are wrong, but I am not arguing that they should be ignored. We need to be very clear and careful about this: we must expand the numbers of those involved in public decision making, not contract it. So what is at stake here is a way of reinventing our democracy so that it is properly deliberative – using argument and discussion to seek viable outcomes – and that it seeks to be persuasive rather than dismissive. The election of 21 May 2022 was a major step in that direction, but it was just one step. There is still a lot of work to be done.

As I've noted, not everything about neoliberalism was bad, nor was everything the Morrison government did. Power and control are never seamless. Even during periods of chronic incompetence there can be moments of smooth sailing, and rarely in life are there absolutes. But there are trends, and what we can say with some confidence, and with the added support of an extraordinary election result on 21 May 2022, is that enough people in Australia had become fed up with the way things were *trending* that they were willing to vote for an altered political order. Not just a change of government, I stress, but the emergence of a new normal in the way we understand Australian democracy. That shift in power went beyond the collapse of the Liberal Party itself and affected other pillars of power within Australian society, particularly the media, and that is what we will look at in the next chapter.

3

Beyond two-party politics and the captured state

The longed-for tidal wave
Of justice can rise up,
And hope and history rhyme.

Seamus Heaney

By week five of the six-week campaign, the 2022 federal election had become a miserable pantomime orchestrated by an image-obsessed prime minister, with a media focused on gotchas and race-call type coverage. Everything people hated about politics and political reporting was being acted out on the national stage and it was as if those involved had no control over their actions. But suddenly the campaign ignited around the issue of a wage increase for Australia's lowest-paid workers. The moment was like one of those heist movies where the cat burglar breaks into the museum and sprays the air to reveal the invisible lines of power that crisscross the space between the door and the display cabinet. Our protagonist then negotiates the journey with balletic movements, trying not to trip the alarm.

Except, for once, Labor leader Anthony Albanese wasn't willing to dance.

He strode across the room, announcing to the assembled media that he 'absolutely' supported a 5.1 per cent pay increase via the Fair Work Commission, and as he did so, the crisscrossing lines of power in Australia lit up and set alarm bells ringing. In unison, key sections of the media, along with all known employer groups, and of course the Liberal–National Party government led by Scott Morrison, rose as one to ward off the threat, the very suggestion that a wage rise was possible.

It was an incredible illustration of how vested interests rally to protect themselves, and it speaks to the way in which the status quo works to hold the rest of us hostage. From Scott Morrison down, the instruments of Australian political and financial power assured us that the pay rise Anthony Albanese was championing threatened to destroy the country. 'It will crush the country' that organ of corporate power, the *Australian Financial Review*, assured us in a headline, going on to say 'Employers and economists are warning that Labor leader Anthony Albanese's advocacy for pay rises greater than 5 per cent to keep pace with [the] soaring cost of living will crush businesses, fuel inflation, and put upward pressure on interest rates.'

One of the employers himself, billionaire owner of Kennards Self-Storage, Sam Kennard, took to Twitter and foreshadowed capital flight, in the time-honoured tradition. He tweeted, 'It's a global marketplace. Australia already has the highest minimum wage in the world. Increasing wages will see industries increasingly relocate overseas.' Scott Morrison, who had spent much of the campaign boasting that, thanks to his government, Australia was witnessing the most spectacular post-Covid recovery of any nation on earth, now insisted that a wage increase would bring the whole thing down. It was like 'throwing fuel on the fire of rising interest rates and rising cost of living', the prime minister insisted.

And let's be clear, here: the pay rise they were all having conniptions about amounted to – wait for it – about one dollar an hour for the lowest-paid workers in the country. A pay increase from $20.33 an hour to $21.37, meaning an annual wage of around $41K. This was the unbearable burden the ruling class was assuring us would bring the economic roof down on our heads. And all this at a time when the share of national income going to profits instead of wages was at a historic high.

In many ways, this was old-fashioned class politics, a fight between capital and labour. But as important an issue as it was, it had an air of kabuki to it. The pay rise Anthony Albanese was committing to was a bare minimum: Labor wasn't exactly trying to seize the means of production. As many economists and commentators pointed out, the mooted rise amounted to a reduction in real wages, not an increase, because it was below the projected inflation rate. What's more, the pay 'rise' was a pittance compared to the tax cuts for high-wage earners the Morrison government had already legislated, cuts supported by the Labor Party *and* the independents. It was an eloquent example of how the automatic stabilisers of the status quo operate – and let me explain what I mean by that.

The first thing we need to recognise is that political power doesn't manifest only in political parties. There are other sources of power that influence the process, and in Australia, these have remained remarkably consistent since Federation in 1901. In her book *The Idea of Australia*, Julianne Schultz wrote, 'The phrase "culture wars" conjures an arcane dispute between ideological opponents about matters of interpretation and understanding, but at heart there is an undeniable political economy. And in Australia, that comes from the four economic foundation stones: mining, agriculture, banking and their handmaiden, the media.'

Schultz noted that during the pandemic, for instance, there arose a desire among many to take advantage of the moment and re-imagine how everything from policing to healthcare to aged care might be reformed. People started talking about different ways of working, about a flexibility that helped workers rather than employers, about a challenge to the idea that we should work entirely to support an economy, a recognition that we were something more than cogs in the neoliberal machine. There was talk of redefining what we meant by 'essential services' to include, for instance, supermarkets and their minimum-wage employees in any definition, given how vital their work was to keeping us all going during lockdowns and beyond. We were all in this together. A society, not an economy. Kumbaya. We raised welfare payments, literally eliminating poverty, and relaxed the so-called mutual obligations around unemployment benefits. The homeless were housed.

And then it all went away.

The more generous welfare conditions were withdrawn. Homeless people who were given shelter during the worst of the pandemic were returned to the streets. Mutual obligations for job seekers were reinstated. Despite the undeniable improvements these changes had made, the automatic stabilisers of the status quo kicked in. Rather than 'doing things differently', Schultz writes, the whole process was undercut by the fact that 'those with the controlling hand on Australian politics and public life were not keen on informed and nuanced discussion that might require action or disrupt the status quo.'

Such manoeuvres are a form of what I will call 'state capture' – the process by which the role of government becomes influenced by those with the power to pursue particular, self-serving agendas at the expense of the common good.

Former senior public servant John Menadue, writing on his *Pearls and Irritations* website, notes vested interests can 'influence governments in a quite disproportionate way'. He says lobbying 'now represents a growing and serious corruption of good governance and the development of sound public policy', and he quotes Professor Ross Garnaut, who has highlighted the 'diabolical problem' that vested interests brought to bear on public discussion on climate change. He notes that Ken Henry, a former secretary of treasury, has said that he 'can't remember a time in the last 25 years when the quality of public policy debate has been as bad as it is right now'. Menadue then quotes other 'insiders' who are similarly concerned about the effect lobbying is having on public policy:

> [Henry] was followed as Secretary of Treasury by
> Martin Parkinson, who has warned about 'vested
> interests' who seek concessions from government
> at the expense of ordinary citizens. The former
> ACCC Chairman, Graeme Samuel, has cautioned
> that 'A new conga line of rent-seekers is lining up
> to take the place of those that have fallen out of
> favour'. And in referring to opposition to company
> tax and carbon pollution reform policies, Fairfax
> columnist Ross Gittins says: 'Industry lobby groups
> have become less inhibited in pressing private
> interests at the expense of the wider public interest.
> They are ferociously resistant to reform proposals.'

In their book *Rigged: How networks of powerful mates rip off everyday Australians*, Cameron Murray and Paul Frijters document what they call the 'game of mates', the endless movement of individuals between political and corporate worlds. 'Lobbying has grown dramatically in recent years, particularly in Canberra,' they write, and it now 'represents a growing and serious corruption of good governance and the development of sound public policy'.

When Schultz, Menadue and others speak of a status quo, they don't just mean a set of institutions that exercise power in various realms and that persist no matter who forms government. They also mean a set of behaviours so normalised in the way the nation operates that it renders the power involved in its exercise invisible, and we can easily list examples from the public and private sectors showing how this process works. The Reserve Bank can be relied upon to operate monetary policy within certain parameters. The police can be relied upon to deal with protesters in a certain manner. The media will amplify predictable voices and ignore others. Media owners and managers will hire editors who won't need to be told what to publish or what not to publish, who will in turn hire journalists who similarly don't need to be told what to report. The people governments appoint to run various agencies will behave as expected and can be removed if they don't. Politicians in political parties will toe the party line and will repeat it ad absurdum in interview after interview.

Such behaviours are the automatic stabilisers of the status quo. They are the forces of structural support built into the institutions themselves, which means no-one has to activate them. Conflict and competition are their necessary adjuncts and often their role is less to do with resolution, or even with stability, but in allowing *process* to continue. These forces are powerful – that's the point – but we need to recognise that power is never seamless. Exceptions to its control will always exist, not least because, in a democracy, all sources of power must pay lip service to the idea of free choice and public legitimacy. Dissent will be curtailed as much as possible

– as various laws limiting workers' ability to strike or protesters' ability to gather attest – but some dissent must be tolerated if the fundamental democratic nature of society is to be maintained. Even political parties, the most hidebound of democratic institutions, throw up the occasional 'maverick', a member who seems to violate the rules of party conformity, and that aberrant behaviour will be tolerated right up until the point that it isn't. The point is, power doesn't have to be absolute to be powerful: what keeps the status quo in a democracy from tipping over into outright oligarchy is that a balance is maintained between the interests of a powerful few and the democratic many, and that was the unspoken rule that the Morrison government abandoned, as we shall see.

Discussion of political power sometimes brings forth the claim that Labor and the Coalition are the same – a claim often made by those on the left looking for a more radical agenda than the ALP is willing to provide – but this is misleading. As Paul Keating said on the eve of the 1996 federal election, when the government changes, the country changes too, a recognition of the fact that the two major parties – as they once were – have traditionally represented different interests. Certainly, since coming to power, the Albanese government has changed important things, such as scrapping the cashless welfare card; abolishing the Australian Building and Construction Commission; and mandating ten days paid leave for workers experiencing domestic violence. But there has also been continuity in among the change, beginning before the election in Labor's small-target approach, its adoption of policies like, or directly supporting, those of the Morrison government. This is an example of the way these hidden sources of power narrow the range of possible political actions, and so there is broad convergence on tax policy, immigration, education and even climate change, with Labor initially offering only a moderately more ambitious carbon reduction target than the Coalition. Economic policy itself, as well as foreign policy, have, for a generation, been approached in tandem. This bipartisanship belies the ostensible confrontational nature of Australian politics and points to the underlying existence of an establishment power.

Since the election, the Albanese government has availed itself of these stabilisers in some areas, even as it used its new power to enact change in others, and there is nothing contradictory about this. Nor is it necessarily a criticism. After all, the ideal for progressives, for democrats, is not that the whole edifice of political and social power is overturned completely in a single election, but that the systems that stay in place, and the changes that are enacted, move us towards being a fairer, more democratic country; that the status quo works for the good of the many and not just the few. Progressivism, in other words, relies on an underlying continuity, and to abandon that entirely risks empowering authoritarianism. It relies on a sense of moderation to balance the headlong flight into the new, while still being open to the new.

Progressive reform also includes the need for ongoing public support, and Labor Party operatives would argue that you can never get too far ahead of public opinion, and that is certainly true. Even after the 2022 election, Essential polling showed that 49 per cent of people thought Labor was 'too idealistic' in their policy goals. But this line of argument conveniently – and conservatively – overlooks the fact that public opinion is never static and that the job of politics is to help define and inform public opinion, not just act as if it is set in stone. This is the very nature of political deliberation, whether it is conducted at a kitchen table or on the floor of the parliament: that it allows people's views to form in open debate in which all options are canvassed.

At the 2022 election, the new crossbench representatives didn't win enough seats to secure the balance of power in the lower house, but at the very least we saw a consolidation of what we can call a third force in Australian politics, in the form of an increasingly significant Greens presence, along with a collection of independents and small parties who can activate around 30 per cent of the national vote. This third force is an existential threat to the legacy parties, chipping away at their primary vote and their ability to muster a parliamentary majority, and indeed, the Voices Of movement has already ploughed and replanted the electoral fields deep in the heartland seats of the Liberal Party itself. This new force has also reduced the number of questions the official Opposition can ask during Question Time, with the balance now – quite rightly – allocated to the crossbench, reflecting its increased size. In some ways, the Liberals have been relegated to a minor party status, while the balance of power within the Coalition with the Nationals has also shifted drastically. The impact of these changes is nonetheless weakened by the habits of power within our institutions, the automatic stabilisers, particularly those of the media, and this masks the extent of the change that has happened. If the crossbench grew further and had the balance of votes within the parliament – and could maintain it – we would be in the realm of a major transformation.

Increasingly, then, the composition and management of this third force will be the defining argument of Australian politics, and it will test the ability of the status quo to adapt. We are already seeing the way in which traditional sources of power, including the Labor Party, are trying to position themselves within this new normal, and to appreciate the direction in which this might all develop, it helps to look at the forces that brought things to a head in the election of 2022. Why were Australians losing faith in the two-party system and choosing to trust their votes to independents and smaller party candidates?

A key factor was that, more than any government before it, the Morrison government was *anti*-government – by which I mean, they consciously neglected obligations most people still thought of as being the job of government, and this neglect was central to the concerns that encouraged people to vote for change on 21 May. The list of failures is long, but they include the fact that Scott Morrison skipped off to Hawaii during the bushfires; failed to order vaccines for Covid in a timely manner; failed to distribute relief funds in the wake of the bushfires, despite making a song and dance about having *set aside* such funding; and was indifferent to the provision of rapid antigen test kits (RATs) as Omicron ran rampant at the end of 2021. None of these were isolated examples of a prime minister flustered or incompetent – they were examples of a prime minister consciously deciding, in line with his underlying beliefs, that people should look after themselves and that, as much as possible, the private sector should do what we have traditionally understood governments to do in these circumstances. If 'the market' failed to step in, then, oh well, individuals, families, communities would just have to take care of themselves. Neoliberalism had already taken us in this direction through outsourcing of government services, privatisation and the elevation of competition as the driving force of policy formation, and to a large extent such practices had become part of the status quo understanding of governance in Australia. But what Morrison was doing was more extreme, and it gave people pause.

We saw the problem writ large when then Defence Minister Peter Dutton organised a private, online fund-raiser (through the GoFundMe platform) for Queensland flood victims rather than enacting federal government support. When challenged on this, Scott Morrison said that he didn't see the problem: 'That sounds to me like someone doing their job. I don't understand the criticism.'

His response perfectly captured the privatised vision of governance Morrison embodied, and it wasn't just an insight into his anti-government values, but an example of how he sought to normalise such values, defining a minister involved in such a private action as 'someone doing their job'.

Evidence of Scott Morrison's belief in this privatised approach to governance went back even further, to when he was Minister for Social Services. In 2015, he told an ACOSS conference that welfare had to be good for business:

> What I am basically saying is that welfare must become a good deal for investors – for private investors. We have to make it a good deal – for the returns to be there, to attract the level of capital that will be necessary in addition to the significant injection of capital and resources that is already provided by States and the Commonwealth.
> *If you have a go, you get a go.*
> *It's not a race.*
> *I don't hold a hose, mate.*

His views were hiding in plain sight, but he also went to extraordinary lengths to disguise them. Just as John Howard supported the neoliberal disruption of the material conditions of a stable society with ever more rhetorical emphasis on the traditional family, Scott Morrison supported his do-nothing approach to government with PR stunts that made it look like he was doing something. He had a personal staff of 51 in the Office of Prime Minister and Cabinet, and ten of them were employed as media advisers. This performative aspect of his prime ministership, the endless and relentless production of photographs and videos of the prime minister cooking a curry, building a cubby house, washing someone's hair; the hi-vis-wearing visits to worksites around the country; the photos of him being given a red carpet welcome by the Air Force; images of him doing 'tours' of bushfire-affected towns and shaking people's hands, whether they wanted to or not – all of these stunts, illusions and advertising were a necessary adjunct to the project of undermining government in which he was engaged.

In other words, we were being railroaded into a diminished understanding and practice of government by a prime minister ideologically opposed to the very idea of government as a bulwark against the risks inherent in a complex society. Our image of ourselves as an egalitarian nation took a hit with every smirk on the prime minister's face, and the rest of the political class, including the media, either kept quiet, perhaps waiting to see what was in it for them, or were openly complicit in the transformation. In doing so, they were violating the key rule that kept the status quo invisible and acceptable. As Canadian writer John Ralston Saul has said: '[Elites] make no sense as a group unless they have a healthy and productive relationship with the rest of the citizenry', and it was becoming apparent that Australia was being stratified in ways that more and more people were finding unacceptable. Saul said that elites, the bearers and beneficiaries of the status quo, 'may prosper far more than the average citizen in the process' and that they 'may have all sorts of advantages', but most people won't care 'so long as the greater interests are also served'.

Scott Morrison's approach to government made it clear that the greater interests would likely never be served, and that he saw government as nothing more than a way of distributing public funds to private providers, whether it was in areas of defence, welfare, or in the response to climate-driven disasters. Indeed, the disasters themselves were a growing source of private profit, and journalist Ben Cubby, in a post-election article in the *Sydney Morning Herald*, noted that 'Private enterprise that specialises in disaster recovery has found a profitable niche by taking on roles that were once assumed by government.' Any doubt that this anti-government approach was the driving logic of Scott Morrison's prime ministership was dispelled two months after his government was thrown from office when he addressed a Pentecostal gathering in Perth in late July, telling the congregation that, 'We trust in Him. We don't trust in governments.'

There was another way in which the Morrison government was threatening the delicate balance between the status quo and the national interest. Political corruption was increasing too, and people's concerns were heightened by the fact that Scott Morrison not only refused to instigate a federal body to investigate these concerns – breaking an election promise – but went so far as to dismiss the successful NSW Independent Commission Against Corruption (ICAC) as a 'kangaroo court'. No wonder Stephen Rushton SC, one of three independent commissioners, dismissed his comments as 'offensive, misleading and untrue'. Rushton called critics such as Morrison 'buffoons'. There was a long list of other problems too, across a range of government departments and instrumentalities, and although many were investigated, political accountability was lacking, and it is worth going through some examples to illustrate the scale of the problem.

Robodebt became the shorthand for a debt recovery scheme implemented through Centrelink. The idea was that, via an online compliance intervention (OCI), people's welfare claims would be matched, via an automated process (an algorithm), against their tax records. This would show up any anomalies between welfare received and other declarations of income. Unfortunately, the automated system was so badly designed and implemented that it produced a huge number of 'false positives', sending people warnings of non-existent overpayments, a failing compounded by the Morrison government's unwillingness to intervene and fix things. In fact, the government almost seemed happy to let the errors run as a way of disciplining welfare recipients in general, and discouraging people from seeking government assistance in the first place. Then minister Alan Tudge threatened those he called welfare cheats: 'We'll find you, we'll track you down, and you will have to repay those debts and you may end up in prison,' he said on the television program *A Current Affair*, and allowed no possibility that there was a fault with the system.

A Senate committee report, *Accountability and justice: Why we need a Royal Commission into Robodebt*, published in May 2022, found that the scheme 'impacted hundreds of thousands of people and, for many, resulted in devastating emotional and psychological harm. It has undermined many people's financial security as well as their willingness to engage with and trust government services.' The report linked the debt recovery scheme to at least three suicides, adding that 'it is not clear how many more may also be linked to the program.' The scheme raised '$1.73 billion in illegitimate debts ... against approximately 433 000 Australians,' and the report notes that 'approximately 381 000 [of these] individuals were pursued, often through private debt collection agencies, to repay almost $752 million to the Commonwealth.' This pursuit would likely have continued had not 'the Federal Court of Australia confirmed that the Government had no legal basis for pursuing these debts.'

I was going to say it would hard to think of a more egregious failure of governance, but unfortunately that's not true.

The Royal Commission into the aged care sector found a similar level of neglect of good governance, and a year before they released their final report, Commissioners Tony Pagone and Lynelle Briggs had already criticised the Morrison government for failing to properly monitor Covid outbreaks in aged care facilities, saying that had 'the Australian government acted upon previous reviews of aged care, the persistent problems in aged care would have been known much earlier and the suffering of many people could have been avoided.' A year later, the Royal Commission's interim report stated that the aged care sector, a federal government responsibility, was 'besieged by neglect'. They noted that substandard care was widespread and that this 'reflects both poor quality on the part of some aged care providers and fundamental systemic flaws with the way the Australian aged care system is designed and governed'. They concluded that 'People receiving aged care deserve better' and the 'Australian community is entitled to expect better.' They made 148 recommendations for reform, and the Morrison government accepted, in full or in part, 126 of them, rejecting a number of key reforms. A year after the report was presented, one of its authors, former commissioner Lynelle Briggs, told the *Sydney Morning Herald* and *The Age* that 'the response should have been better'.

But perhaps no issue better illustrates the way in which the Morrison government corrupted normal processes of governance than the way in which they directed special payments to certain electorates, seats they wished to 'pork barrel' to assist their own electoral chances. Many in the media insisted that such funding anomalies were as old as politics itself, and that both sides were guilty of such behaviour, but there is no doubt that in doing so these journalists were not comparing like with like, and the 'both sides' approach in their reporting acted to stabilise state power, rather than challenging it, as the 'fourth estate' is meant to do.

So yes, most governments engage in some form of funding for different electorates, and there have no doubt been instances where all parties have played favourites, but the Morrison government took the practice to an unprecedented level of partisan advantage. The 2020 report by the Australian National Audit Office (ANAO) into $100 million dollars' worth of funds provided as grants to various sporting organisations around the country found that the 'award of grant funding was not informed by an appropriate assessment process and sound advice'. It noted that 'the program was deficient in a number of important areas' and that 'a significant shortcoming was that, while the program guidelines identified that the Minister for Sport would approve CSIG [Community Sport Infrastructure Grant] funding, there are no records evidencing that the Minister was advised of the legal basis on which the Minister could undertake an approval role, and it is not evident to the ANAO what the legal authority was.'

Tell me something is illegal without calling it illegal.

Further, the ANAO found that the 'Minister's Office drew upon considerations other than those identified in the program guidelines, such as the location of projects, and also applied considerations that were inconsistent with the published guidelines', and that this 'resulted in the assessment advice to the Minister being inconsistent with the approved program guidelines.' Confronted with such findings, the Morrison government not only ignored normal procedures of accountability – and even though Minister for Sport Bridget McKenzie resigned over the matter, she returned to Cabinet a year later – the prime minister himself suggested the process that uncovered this malfeasance was 'autocratic'.

'If we are going to so disempower our elected representatives to do things about what is needed in their communities, then what is the point?' the prime minister asked reporters. 'We can't just hand government over to faceless officials to make decisions that impact the lives of Australians from one end of the country to the other. I actually think there's a great danger in that. It wouldn't be Australia anymore if that was the case, it would be some kind of public autocracy.'

Take a moment and let that sink in.

This was the prime minister defining the normal operation of democratic oversight as a 'public autocracy', arguing that all spending decisions should be taken, unencumbered, by individual politicians, which – is 'paradoxically' the right word here? – is the normal definition of autocracy (rule by an individual).

As an argument, it is incoherent, but it served his purpose of redefining democratic practice as autocratic and ministerial fiat as legitimate. So, just as he had described the NSW ICAC as a 'kangaroo court', he was now suggesting that any sort of public oversight of government spending was autocratic. It spoke to a level of contempt for normal democratic processes that was deeply concerning, and I think it is fair to say that such views characterised his entire approach to government. We saw it again in a review of the public service in the wake of the 2019 election, when he made it clear that he did not want policy advice from public servants, just compliance around the government's agenda. 'That is why under our system of government,' he said, 'it must be ministers who set the policy direction.'

Such comments took on a more sinister tone when it was revealed in August 2022, three months after the election, that Scott Morrison had, as prime minister, assumed the role of at least five other ministerial portfolios. He had had himself sworn into these ministries, and the move was not only unprecedented but undisclosed, even to most of his Cabinet colleagues. In a press conference on 17 August, he justified his behaviour as a fallback position in case of unforeseen events arising from the circumstances of the pandemic, and as unconvincing an explanation as that was, it reinforced the increasingly emerging image of him, even among colleagues, as power-hungry. Liberal senator Concetta Fierravanti-Wells had, after all, called him the most ruthless person she had dealt with, saying '[He] is not interested in rules-based order. It is his way or the highway. An autocrat, a bully who has no moral compass.'

And wait, there's more.

The Royal Commission into the banking industry found similar failings of governance. The Royal Commission itself only came about because of excellent investigative reporting, including by Adele Ferguson, and her book *Banking Bad* sets out the ways in which the sector worked within the hidden networks of power that determine how Australia is governed:

The banks' powers rested not just in the profound wealth they were probably producing, but also in the deep connection between the banks and the political establishment. Former heads of treasury, premiers, Reserve Bank governors, ASIC commissioners and ministerial advisers had all joined their ranks, taking up seats on boards and other key positions of influence [so that the] meshing of the political class into the finance sector both reflects the power of the banks and in turn contributes to the power of the banks.

It is one thing for a nation to have underlying sources of power that maintain themselves no matter who is in government, but increasingly Australia was moving towards a more dangerous and distorted version of this 'state capture'. According to the World Bank, state capture is 'the exercise of power by private actors – through control over resources, threat of violence, or other forms of influence – to shape policies or implementation in service of their narrow interests'. The point is, it isn't just a case of out-and-out corruption, but relationships that develop over years that distort good governance – that is, governance in the interests of the many and not the few. A report out of South Africa in 2018 noted that state capture is 'systemic and well organised by people who have an established relationship with one another. It involves repeated transactions, often on an increasing scale.'

Corruption, in other words, isn't always illegal.

Another major report called *Confronting State Capture*, written by the Australian Democracy Network, including former Greens senator Scott Ludlam, highlighted many of the ways in which government and business directly and indirectly colluded and worked against the interests of the common good. They looked at case studies in the fossil fuel industries and the arms industries and uncovered disturbing practices that had become normalised. The report noted that the exercise of such power happened in well-defined ways, and there were clearly established practices of lobbying, political donations, and even public attack campaigns operated by well-funded front groups that advanced individual and sectorial interests. In a January 2022 report, *Selling Out: How powerful industries corrupt our democracy*, produced by the Human Rights Law Centre, the authors high-lighted all these methods, and argued that 'Corporate influence in our politics is distorting our democratic processes', and that we 'need to hit reset on our democracy and reform our laws to ensure our politicians respond to voters, not vested corporate interests'.

The bottom line is that while we might be able to vote out any given government – we are still a demo-cracy, after all – certain networks endure, and even if we have ostensible checks and balances in place to ensure accountability, these will not be enough if the government of the day can't be relied on to use them. Certainly, Australians felt that the Morrison government was failing in this regard, and there were other areas in which people felt their country slipping away from them.

In this context, it is important to examine the role of the political media, because they are the most enduring and essential of the automatic stabilisers. Schultz rightly called them the handmaiden of all the other 'foundation stones' of political power in the country, which belies the media's self-generated image as a check on power. They *can* be that – as the banking example above shows – but often they are captured by these other sources of power. Journalist Margaret Simons (paraphrasing historian Mitchell Stephens) noted in an article in *Meanjin* that 'the role of the media in relatively free Western societies is mostly cohesive, and supportive of the status quo … At most it may be a force for reform and often it is not even that.' What's more, Stephens noted, the media covered its support for the status quo by producing 'an occasional exposé'. It is a devastating accusation, suggesting they do just enough to maintain a façade of ruthless investigation while in fact spending most of their time stabilising establishment power.

The problems in Australian media go deep, from concentration of ownership to the deployment of tropes and practices that are well past their use-by date. Often, it is as if they had failed to notice – or refused to accept – that the top-down, unidirectional, mass nature of political reporting had been transformed into a multidirectional, fragmented and niche environment in which the audience was no longer a passive recipient but an active participant in the creation and distribution of news. Their outdated approach and the concomitant hostility of many in the media towards their own audiences – especially as they manifested on various platforms of social media – pervaded the way the 2022 election was covered, and it was a particularly profound betrayal because, against all odds, Australian democracy was in the midst of a renaissance, and it was as if the media couldn't see what was in front their nose.

Not all media, I hasten to add. But my god, a lot of them.

The emergence of the Voices Of candidates in electorates all around the country, culminating in the unprecedented rise of the 'teal' candidates in the 2022 election, spoke to a nation taking seriously the need for democratic renewal, trying to push back against the state capture increasingly apparent in everything from how politics was conducted to how it was reported. As we have seen, these independents generated huge community support from a standing start by engaging in the sort of grassroots campaigning that is the heart and soul of democracy, and they, and we-the-people, deserved better than a media wallowing in the sort of cynicism and once-over-easy approach that pervaded so much election reporting.

Journalists love to say that voters are disengaged from the political process, but who is really disengaged?

The digitisation of news had changed the way news in general, and politics in particular, was reported, and the old static model of appointment television and deadline-sensitive front pages was still being imposed on a media environment that was much more fluid. The logic of *paper* still held in newsrooms, and editors at *The Age* and the *Sydney Morning Herald* still ran images of their newspaper front pages on Twitter as if these remnants of the era of the printing press were a viable organising tool of contemporary journalism. It was a practice that spoke to a deeper disconnect between journalists and their audiences, and it was part of the reason social media itself was so important to the rise of the independents. As BBC reporter Ros Atkins argued recently:

> News is not a given in people's lives. It can't be assumed people will seek to learn about our world via journalism. It can't be assumed that the way we tell stories is the way people want to hear them. Our place in people's lives is not a guarantee. And so, when I look at the need to innovate, to reimagine, to restructure what we do – it's not because change is fun and creative and exciting … For me this is a necessity. If you believe in the importance of journalism to our society – and to the world – then actively engaging in what we need to become isn't optional. This isn't some distant moment.

All this is true, and the technical reform and changes to storytelling that Atkins talks about are important to consider. But the bottom line is that the media have lost our trust. The 2022 election showed their ability to dictate the terms of an election had diminished, and they risk painting themselves into a corner of increasing irrelevance. Nonetheless, in a piece in *Meanjin* written during the election, I suggested that rumours of the death of media influence were exaggerated; that they still wielded what I called soft power, so that even when they were unable to change minds directly with a given article or series of articles, they nonetheless constrained the sorts of conversations that we could conduct.

My point was that our existence is mediated more than we like to admit, to an extent we generally don't notice: the perfect example of the automatic stabilisers doing their silent work. To help us control the information that saturates our every waking moment, we rely on mental shortcuts, heuristics, and everyone from advertisers to politicians leans into these shortcuts to reinforce their preferred version of reality. In politics, this is why easily demonstrable falsehoods persist: that the Coalition are better economic managers; that working-class means men in factories and high-vis vests; that deficits are always bad. It is easier to regurgitate received wisdom than to pick it apart. It is more agreeable to maintain our prejudices than to see past them. The status quo is always going to status quo. It is why, as Winston Churchill said, a lie gets halfway around the world before truth puts on its boots.

When we talk about the power of the media, then, this is how we should be thinking about it: not that a single article or newsclip is going to sway people one way or another, but that the media help create an overall environment that boxes us into certain ways of thinking. The box is never completely airtight, and other institutions build their own boxes, but the media

– broadly understood – help maintain strict perimeters around our thinking about almost everything. That is the nature of its power, and it exists independently of whatever industry statistics say about audience levels or profitability.

As Julianne Schultz argued, the media is just one player in a much bigger political economy of information and ideas, and so the point isn't just that certain media outlets might be little more than the propaganda wing of the Liberal–National Party Coalition – as true as that might be – but that the whole history of Australian media is inextricably tied to the interests of capital. Melbourne University academic Sally Young's immense work on the early history of Australian media, *Paper Emperors*, shows that Australian newspapers have been consistently anti-Labor, even anti-*labour*, which in turns speaks to the conservative nature of the status quo more generally and its class composition:

> By the late 19th century, Australia was developing a reputation for being a 'working man's paradise'. Australia's conservative newspaper owners were concerned about the effects of demands for improved working conditions on the profitability of industries that many were now heavily invested in – including mining, retail, production, agriculture and, of course, the newspaper industry.

She writes that on the formation of the Labor Party, the *Sydney Morning Herald* described 'the intrusion ... of the labour struggle into the field of politics' as the nation's 'greatest peril'. Young even suggests that the concept of the 'fourth estate', the idea of the media as a watchdog on power, was nothing more than a cover to ensure that any partisanship they showed didn't discourage advertising. 'The concept of political independence that underpinned the "fourth estate" was so central to the identity of newspapers that it had to be vehemently proclaimed even when there was much evidence to the contrary.' And the evidence of anti-Labor bias is overwhelming:

> This book concludes in 1941, with Menzies'
> resignation, but the political stances of the
> newspapers need to be viewed in a longer context to
> see how determinedly conservative the mainstream
> daily press was, and would remain for decades.
> From 1922 until 1969, the majority of daily
> newspapers were conservative … especially in the
> 1920s–40s, when 85–90 per cent of commercial
> dailies supported the conservative parties … Even
> up to the 1960s, Labor never received the support
> of a quarter of the Australian daily press … Instead,
> for five decades, the conservative parties could
> count on the backing of a core group of papers that
> always directed their readers to vote conservative.
> This group included: the *Mercury*, the *Herald*,
> the *Sun News-Pictorial*, the *Advertiser*, the *West
> Australian*, and from its formation in 1933, the
> *Courier-Mail*.

Young continues by saying, 'To this group of core conservative papers can also be added the *Daily Telegraph*, which never advocated a vote for Labor during this period', and that 'The *Sydney Morning Herald* must also be included because it opposed Labor at every election except one – 1961. Likewise, the *Sun* only supported Labor once, also in 1961, and that was because it was the *Sydney Morning Herald*'s stablemate by then, so it was ensnared in the Fairfax group's anti-Menzies campaign that year.' She points out that even when Labor won its sweeping victory in 1983 under Bob Hawke, *The Age* was the only paper to endorse the ALP. Her work is a useful reminder of the hill Labor must climb at every election when the mainstream media is implacably opposed to the idea of it forming government. Even today, the former Fairfax papers, known now as Nine Entertainment, have a retired senior Liberal politician as their chairman, and an editor at the *Sydney Morning Herald* whom internal documents reveal insisted on reporting a lockout of railway staff by the Liberal NSW government as a strike by the workers – about as egregious a misreporting of facts as you could imagine, even if the 'error' was eventually acknowledged in a begrudging note to subscribers.

American philosopher Hannah Arendt once wrote that 'Facts need testimony to be remembered and trustworthy witnesses to be established in order to find a secure dwelling place in the domain of human affairs', and in any definition of public interest journalism, this role as 'trustworthy witness' is central. What became apparent during the 2022 election was that the power of the mainstream to influence voters had diminished, and that this was part of a more general failure of the industry to fulfil their role as a trusted witness to events.

What was remarkable about the period leading up to the 2022 election was not just that political news media were failing in this way, but that many more people than usual were willing to say so. This included a lot of journalists, many of whom had either retired or been made redundant in the downsizing of the industry apparent since at least the 1980s, or who had set up shop as freelancers or independent journalists with their own websites and social media presences. Respected journalists such as Michael West, Barrie Cassidy, Eleanor Hall, Peter Clarke, Margo Kingston, Chris Wallace, Jonathan Green, Bronwyn Clark, Rachel Withers, Laura Tingle, Virginia Trioli, Nick Bryant and Geoff Kitney criticised former and current employers and the industry in general. Former prime ministers Kevin Rudd (Labor) and Malcolm Turnbull (Liberal) openly called for a Royal Commission into News Corp and used social media to document the abuses of media power they were concerned about.

The problem wasn't just out-and-out bias, though there was plenty of evidence of that. It was more that large sections of the political media had become reliant on the government for access to information, often provided in the form of what were called 'drops', a particularly dangerous form of state capture. To stay on this teat, journalists and editors tended to present stories in a way that rarely held the government properly to account. Again, there was nothing new in this. As far back as … well, forever, journalists have relied on insider relationships to feed their stories. In 2013, Matthew Knott wrote in *Crikey* that such stories 'nearly always involve a simple proviso: the journalist does not approach third parties for comment before publication.' He added that, in theory, 'it's a win–win scenario. The journalist gets an "exclusive". The politician gets clear air for his or her policy, at least for a few hours, before opponents start tearing it apart.' But the key point was what this chummy arrangement meant for the reader. Aren't they being cheated by this sort of news management?

'Oh yes!' replied one press gallery reporter he spoke with. 'From a reader's point of view, it's awful. You haven't served your reader well, but you wouldn't be serving your reader well if you didn't get the information.'

By the time of the Morrison government, as with many such matters, practices like drops had been weaponised. In the same publication in 2019, Christopher Warren wrote:

> There's little more irresistible in political reporting than the well-timed leak. It's the perfectly crafted win–win of the outside–insider model of reporting that shapes modern journalism: a story (a scoop!) for the journalist, political advantage to the leaker with a profile lifted or a news cycle launched.
> Now, under Morrison and his loyal team in the Prime Minister's Office, it's been gamed out to its end point. No longer about getting the news out,

governmental leaks have been turned into a potent political weapon with a single goal: to damage, to deflect, to mislead.

Then there was what was happening at the ABC.

There is an entire book to be written about the collapse in standards at shows like *7.30*, *Insiders*, and *Q&A*, but, at the very least, large parts of the ABC had been captured not just by state power – who provided their funding and used threats of cuts, and actual cuts, as leverage – but by the power of the Murdoch press. The ABC endlessly platformed News Corp journalists on their various radio and television programs, and constantly fell back on Murdoch news stories to frame their own work. The 'what the papers say' segment many ABC programs ran became – inevitably, given the continued dominance of News Corp in that sector – nothing more than a recitation of Murdoch news talking points, a bleeding of the News Corp worldview into nearly every aspect of political reporting on the national broadcaster. At the editorial level, at the level of the producer, many in the ABC were in a News Corp state of mind. And this included an open hostility to the most engaged part of their audience that regularly commented upon and discussed politics on social media, on Twitter in particular.

All this culminated in 2022 in what was arguably the most appalling election campaign coverage in living memory. It was a disgrace to the profession of journalism and a stain on our democracy. It began on the opening day with a collective freak-out by journalists about Anthony Albanese's 'gaffe' – when he couldn't recall a few key economic statistics – and continued to the tantrum six weeks later when the Opposition leader suggested the media pack could listen to Shadow Treasurer Jim Chalmers talk about budget costings rather than follow him (Albanese) to Queensland. Throughout the campaign, the media behaved with all the grace and subtlety of rival gangs of mobsters discussing security arrangements at a new pizza joint.

The entire methodology of how elections were covered, it became obvious, was broken, and many of those entrusted with reporting on this most important event in the cycle of democracy were either not up to the task or so constrained by riding orders from head office that the entire process turned into a farce. And these riding orders are key, I think, because whatever abilities and knowledge individual journalists may have brought to the task at hand, editors with agendas demanded that certain matters and approaches be foregrounded, and they often emphasised confrontation over nuance; fluff over substance. In an interview in which I asked a number of journalists about what they thought audiences didn't understand about the way journalism worked, Margo Kingston told me that 'One big thing that people don't understand is that head office is very directive. They know what they want and they're looking for a package.' By which she meant a neatly wrapped-up story, or range of stories, to present to an audience. How else to explain the puerile piece – written by the *Sydney Morning*

Herald's 'national affairs editor' and passed off as 'analysis' – that contained this statement: 'If Jenny Morrison could meet 50.1 per cent of voters, Scott Morrison would be prime minister for life'?

Consider the chain of failure, from conception to editing to publication, needed to allow that sentence to see the light of day. It was obviously part of the sort of package Kingston highlighted.

Nine had a particularly bad election, their credibility not helped by the fact that their chair was Peter Costello, a former Liberal Party deputy leader and federal treasurer – a classic example of how state capture works, as various individuals shift seamlessly between government and the private sector. Nine exposed their vulnerability to such criticisms when, for instance, *The Age* ran an 'editor's pick' story prominently on their website that included a photo of Treasurer Josh Frydenberg shaking hands with … Peter Costello. This troubling conflict of interest was airily waved away in the story as nothing more than a coincidence.

Meanwhile, the *Sydney Morning Herald* leaned into stories about Katherine Deves, the candidate Scott Morrison had personally installed in the seat of Warringah and who ran on an anti-trans agenda. The stories were not just presented with an emphasis damaging to trans people themselves – as many noted on social media – but one that bolstered an obvious tactic of distraction and dog-whistling orchestrated by the prime minister and his office.

Nine's biggest failure, though, was the so-called leaders' debate, which, in the absence of any real attempt to stick to a format or maintain balance, descended into a shouting match. As if that wasn't bad enough, one of the debate participants, Nine's political editor, Chris Uhlmann, spent the next few days, and thousands of words, pompously telling everyone that the debate was in fact great, an ornament to public interest journalism, and who are you going believe, him or your lying eyes? The editor of the *Sydney Morning Herald*, Bevan Shields, mocked people on Twitter (that is, members of his own audience) and tweeted sarcastically that he was 'shocked to see Twitter and some competitors bagging last night's debate'. He then linked to a story by one of his own journalists, David Crowe, which he described as a 'sensible take'.

The contempt for the audience in all this was palpable.

And it was embedded in the deeper problem of campaign coverage itself, with its media buses and set-piece confrontations in front of a never-ending list of preordained backdrops. The notion that after three years of government – in fact, the LNP had been in power for nine years – the process of an election could be reduced to a highly confected and tightly managed four-to-six-week performance piece – a campaign – was in and of itself damaging to the notion of democratic accountability. But some journalists sought to defend the unedifying performance of the daily press conferences on the grounds that the politicians had been light-on with policy, thus 'forcing' journalists into trivia and gotchas. Nick McCallum from Channel Seven tweeted that 'Albo's "small target" policy' had backfired. 'With so few substantive policies announced, attention invariably turns to other issues, in his case, to leadership and lack of attention to detail. If you want debates of substance, give voters substance.' He was supported in this dubious line of reasoning by *Age* journalist Chip Le Grand, who tweeted that 'If either party was offering a serious policy choice, they would get more serious policy questions. Just saying.' Former News Corp journalist Malcolm Farr, in what was an otherwise reasonable piece published on the Judith Neilson Foundation website, noted that 'the heavily structured yet lightweight Morrison and Albanese campaigns [relied] on selling an image rather than detailed policy.'

The argument missed the bigger point, which was the fact that whatever the failures of the politicians, it didn't mitigate the media's own failures. Saying that the media were bad because the politicians were bad didn't address the problem – it doubled it. The entire campaign process highlighted the toxic, co-dependent relationship between journalists and politicians, where each relied on the other for support. The whole culture of 'drops' and strategic leaks, with the concomitant creation of hierarchies, where politicians had favoured journalists they could rely on to present information in a way that favoured them, was a cancer on our democracy and fatal to the very notion of journalism as a fourth estate, as a check on power, as a trustworthy witness.

It was hardly surprising, given all this, that the rise of the 'teal' independents was (and is) viewed by the political class as a threat. As the election unfolded, it was staggering the extent to which the mainstream parties and the mainstream media – the broad political class – were hostile to the independents and smaller parties. It spoke to the sense of entitlement cultivated in the media environment I've been describing, one that allowed that class to believe the two-party system was sacrosanct and their right to govern was a given. It wasn't just the unseemly childishness of candidates like Josh Frydenberg, Tim Wilson and Dave Sharma, whining about 'fake independents' who dared to challenge them. Nor was it the predictable hostility of both major parties pompously announcing they would not deal with an elected crossbench of small parties and independents in the event of a minority government. It was also the way in which a particular bias was built into the very fabric of how the media thought about politics.

This was highlighted in a letter the independent member for Warringah, Zali Steggall, sent the ABC. She pointed out that the ABC's popular 'Vote Compass' – which allowed people to answer questions about parties and policies and thus place themselves on a grid indicating whether they were left or right economically, and progressive or conservative socially – ignored entirely the existence of the independent position:

> I currently hold the seat of Warringah with a
> margin of 7.2 percent, and yet on Vote Compass,
> none of my constituents will be able to indicate
> their intention to vote for me as the survey currently

stands … I also note that in the policy section of the survey, there is no question about a federal integrity commission, which is a central plank of my policy platform and a key issue at this election.

In the end, Scott Morrison lost the 2022 election, but given his track record and basic unfitness for the job – a fact increasingly admitted by people on his own side of politics – the only reason he remained in contention was because of the media's ability to present him and his government in such a way as to seem legitimate and to cast doubt upon all alternatives. Sections of the media threw everything they had at the independents, at the Greens and at Labor, and lauded the Morrison government at every point, but at the end of the day their propaganda was ignored, and the Liberals lost their heartland.

Still, media power isn't always about the ability to dominate. It can be enough to maintain a sufficient hold on the conversation to keep underlying power intact. We happily talk about the importance of 'soft power' in the projection of our interests in foreign policy, but we are just as susceptible to it at home, and the media remain the primary tool for the dissemination of that power. They remain the most visible purveyors of the otherwise invisible power that helps maintain the status quo.

In this regard, News Corp in Australia remains a central problem, its mastheads and cable news outlet having well and truly gone down the path first trodden by their sister organisation in the United States, Fox News, of open agitation in favour of one side of politics.

As journalist and educator Margaret Simons has written, News Corp is a news organisation in name only and '[it] is time to stop pretending otherwise.' She notes that there are still 'excellent journalists employed by News Corporation [but the] merits of the good reporting and analysis are more than countered by intense, politically charged campaigns against institutions and individuals, sometimes with inadequate respect for the facts.'

Given this, it is deeply disappointing – but in terms of an analysis of power, not at all surprising – that the Albanese government has already announced that it will not be pursuing any sort of media inquiry, let alone the Royal Commission into News Corp that Kevin Rudd and Malcolm Turnbull have called for. 'I have ruled out a royal commission into News Corporation,' Anthony Albanese told a News Corp journalist in an exclusive interview before the election. 'At this point, I can't see a case for any other regulation or inquiries. Clearly media policy won't stay the same forever and we would deal with that on a case-by-case basis. At this stage, I don't envisage anything being on the immediate horizon.' In late June 2022, this stance was confirmed by Michelle Rowland, the new Communications Minister, and she made it clear that the government's priority was to make sure the legacy media organisations were given every assistance in reaching audiences by making sure that they were easily available through smart TVs. 'This is a priority area, and it has been described by some of the free-to-air broadcasters as the most pressing issue they have,' she said. 'It's about ensuring that Australian content including news and important information is capable of being found.' It was a classic example of how the status quo is maintained, with government shaping policy around the needs of a given industry.

The new government was also considering funding regional, community and specialist services, including Indigenous media outlets, but the relative amounts involved indicate the way in which legacy organisations – the handmaidens of the status quo – are always given a leg-up.

There are some bursts of hopeful life in the sector, particularly in the rise, in Australia, of the *Guardian* – unburdened as it by the logic and reality of having to create a 'newspaper' every day and existing only online. There is also *The Conversation*, perhaps the best media start-up of the last 30 years, launched in Australia and now running in seven other countries. There has also been the resurrection of the Australia Associated Press (AAP), which brings an imperfect but welcome breath of non-partisanship to its journalism.

But overall, the prognosis is not great.

There are obvious improvements that could be made to political coverage, especially during elections, and journalist Ben Eltham tweeted suggestions ranging from abandoning the idea of a bus full of journalists following politicians around on the campaign trail, to making sure that journalists with policy knowledge were the ones asking the policy questions. It was not the first time someone had made such a list – Margo Kingston had been arguing against the campaign bus since the Hanson elections of the late 1990s – and the fact that we were still having the discussion two decades later showed just how resistant to change the industry was. Like the old joke, the lightbulb must want to change, and neither of the parties to the ongoing farce of election campaigns – the political parties and the mainstream media – seemed remotely interested in changing things.

Serious media reform requires not just ongoing funding for new outlets, but a complete rethink of the relationship between media and audiences. New sources of funding for mainstream media such as the Judith Neilson Foundation, and the ACCC media code that forced Google and Facebook to pay certain news organisations, have helped keep these organisations from slipping down the drain they were already circling, but they have done little to improve the quality of the journalism itself. What is really needed is internal reform, and that is unlikely to happen if governments, philanthropists and consumers keep throwing good money after bad, rewarding mere existence rather than actual change. The now-abandoned inquiry into News Corp was a missed opportunity to demand some accountability.

Frankly, after more than 20 years of watching and analysing the industry, writing books and endless articles about what ails the sector, having been on endless panels and engaged in endless exchanges with well-meaning and not-so-well-meaning journalists, having worked in the industry mainly as a freelancer, but also for a number of years at News Limited itself, I find myself reluctantly admitting that I have lost faith in the ability of the industry to reform itself. If the underlying status quo remains intact, there is no real motive for the media to change, and recognising this fact is likely to be the key to meaningful reform. The handmaiden will remain enslaved to the views of the status quo.

Audiences who want to support genuine media reform are better advised to help build a new network of independent outlets sensitive to the concerns of local communities and to the overarching requirements of democracy. The traditional model of public interest journalism would be enhanced with a new emphasis on bottom-up engagement, in the same way as our politics has been. More than ever, then, we need a Voices of Journalism movement, led by journalists themselves – maybe the ones who have already spoken out – but involving audiences as much as they possibly can.

In fact, many of the elements are already in place, and some of those involved in the Voices Of political movement are thinking about ways in which we might proceed. Denise Shrivell, who was involved in the Voices Of North Sydney movement, has already been canvassing ideas for a new media network, built, like the Voices Of movement, from the ground up. 'The overall concept,' she told me, 'is not to create a *new* news media publisher, but to curate the approximately 70 Australian independent news media publishers into one easy-to-access portal or destination.' In this scenario, she suggested, 'we'd create a single curated website which links directly to articles by Australia's 70 independent news media publishers, produce an afternoon e-newsletter listing content produced by independent news media publishers, making indie news media more accessible, rather than [people having to navigate] to 70 individual destinations.'

The 70 individual destinations she speaks of include Michael West Media; the Schwartz media group that includes *The Monthly* and *The Saturday Paper*; *Crikey*; *The Conversation*; sites that specialise in matters to do with political polling and related matters, such as *The Tally Room* and Kevin Bonham's website; well-established sites like *IndigenousX*, *Inside Story*, *Meanjin*, *Pearls and Irritations*, and *Overland Literary Journal* that publish knowledgeable writers with real expertise; and a number of newer sites such as *The Shot* and *In Queensland*.

Another hopeful sign is the local start-up *PS Media, headed up by founding editor of *BuzzFeed Australia*, Simon Crerar, and the former head of Melbourne University's postgraduate school of journalism, Margaret Simons. *PS Media is focused on local news and is employing an innovative business model that allows locals to buy shares in the company. It is in its infancy, but its broad approach of community engagement, working with locals to produce journalism that communities want, is precisely the sort of approach media in general should take – a version of the Voices Of methodology applied to journalism.

Any aggregation of alternative media sites of the sort suggested by Shrivell, then, could not seek to dominate the public sphere in which Australian politics is conducted, nor replace the legacy outlets, but it could force open the window of which topics are debated and how they are debated, and wrest some of that soft power away from the mainstream. The bottom line is that the ability of independent politicians to communicate directly with their communities via newsletters, websites and social media itself will continue to undermine the ability of the legacy media to frame politics and policy, weakening their role as handmaiden to other sources of power within the country. The effects of this sort of structural transformation of the public sphere are likely to be deep and long-lasting.

One thing I am absolutely convinced of is that media reform will not happen among journalists alone; it will only happen with the support of audiences themselves, and is only likely to be successful if conducted within the framework of a Voices Of–type process that audiences themselves help to organise.

For now, we are in a moment of flux, and we won't know until the next election the true significance of the last one. If we watch closely, we can see the way in which political power is evolving, how a new third force is asserting itself, as well as how the status quo is protecting itself in the face of change. This can teach us a lot about the direction in which the country will move in the years ahead, and every decision and response taken now is part of a bigger debate about the sort of country we want to be.

Part Three
In the middle,
somewhat elevated

The past cannot be forgotten,
the present cannot be remembered.

Mark Fisher

4

When the country changes: Reforming democracy for a new era

Not for the first time in history may makeshifts contain the germs of great and permanent institutions.

Karl Polanyi

The election of nine independents and four Greens to the House of Representatives on 21 May 2022 wasn't a revolution – much of the old order remained in place – but it nonetheless represented a significant realignment of power, one that provided a platform for further democratic reform. As we watch the United States struggle with the aftermath of an attempted coup and a constitutional stasis allowing powerful minorities to override the will of the people on everything from gun control to abortion, and as we watch Britain wrestle with the legacy of a still-dominant class system that is threatening its social, political and spiritual coherence, we need to recognise the opportunity we have built for ourselves using the tools of Australian democracy, and make sure we push for further improvements. In fact, Australia may be unique in finding a way of addressing the loss of legitimacy being experienced in established democracies around the world, and the singular achievement of the Voices Of movement has been its reassertion of the democratic right of citizens to participate in their own governance, opening the possibility of reform outside the confines of what the 'major' parties would normally tolerate.

The Greens, too, deserve credit for enacting a community engagement approach, and it is part of this larger transformation. Their success in Queensland was not the result of any last-minute capitalisation on local issues – as defeated Labor candidate Terri Butler complained in a post-election interview – but was the result of long-term planning. Max Chandler-Mather, the Greens candidate who defeated Butler, wrote in *Jacobin* magazine as long ago as 2020 that 'the Queensland Greens' approach isn't premised on a sudden populist surge. Instead, since 2016, [our] plan emphasized patiently and consistently building a movement capable of reaching people, primarily through face-to-face conversations.' The kitchen table discussions and the other public events these community groups created brought local voices together and raised them up. It is an incredible achievement and we should embrace it. Participants rejected the notion that a democracy should consist of insiders and outsiders, and reminded everyone that voting is important but that it isn't enough: people need to be able to have an ongoing say in how the country is run *between elections*. Politicians need to be accountable *every day*, not just on election day.

Many of those involved in what happened in

communities around Australia in the lead-up to the 2022 election saw themselves as 'ordinary Australians', as no-one special, as people occupying some middle ground in the Australian political landscape. From the candidates up, they described themselves as 'centrists' who didn't often stick their heads above the parapet, but who knew they were being left behind. The Voices Of movement listened to this disaffected middle, and elevated their concerns. As a result, Australia moved into an era of third party politics, where that 'third party' consisted of the Greens, independents, and a handful of other smaller parties. The country had been moving in this direction for several years – as the primary vote for the 'major' parties had, election after election, dropped from the high forties into the low thirties – but this was a major consolidation of grassroots power.

Nonetheless, the independents in their various forms, along with a record number of successful Greens candidates, sit on a crossbench that may have a moral imperative to have a say in the governing of the country but doesn't have the numbers, and resolving this disconnect will be central to our politics from here forward.

Prime Minister Anthony Albanese brought a rein-vigorated policy agenda to the parliament on 26 July, the first sitting day of the new era, and many of the items he and his government set out to pursue were welcome. But the real test of his tenure, and of any future prime minister, will not just be the policies they pursue, but the way in which they include the new elevated middle of

Australian politics, as represented by the crossbench in both houses, in the governing process. The complexity and urgency of the problems facing us – and the rest of the world – are such that no single party can claim to have all the answers, and any government that doesn't allow for as broad a consultation as possible is likely dooming us to inadequate responses.

Make no mistake, the automatic stabilisers of the status quo are already doing their work. A concerted effort is being made to negate the change we voted for on 21 May. Amnesia is already being orchestrated. Yes, the government changed, and the country changed with it, and in many ways for the better, but there has still been a worrying reversion to the political mean on key issues. Early polls showed that approval for the Albanese government, and the prime minister himself, had skyrocketed, but this was likely little more than relief that Scott Morrison had gone – it is hard to overestimate how unpopular he had become – and old metrics like this will mislead if we don't take account of the deeper change that has occurred. In fact, assertions of a mandate, instead of a willingness to consult, are only likely to anger those who voted for change. At the same time, the independents need to recognise that the tools that got them elected are not going to be enough to ensure that they can create real reform, while the inherent contradictions in the 'centrism' they espouse is going to leave them vulnerable in other ways.

Let's look at this.

The fact that Labor had a majority of seats in the

new parliament allowed many to fall straight back into the two-party mindset, and most in the media acted as if nothing fundamental had changed, directing their attention to the legacy parties and their prospects. Even when journalists acknowledged the success of independents and smaller parties, they often framed it in terms of its being an aberration, even as a negative, seeing the story through the concerns of the major parties. Witness Andrew Brown from AAP news wire's questioning of Labor's National Secretary, Paul Erickson, at the National Press Club a few weeks after the election. 'We saw a bit of a fundamental shift on election night, with a lot of voters ditching the major parties and instead choosing independents and minor parties,' Brown led. 'What part of Labor strategies going forward would you think would have to change to make sure that safe Labor seats, particularly in inner city areas, *don't suffer a similar fate*?' (My emphasis, his presumption.)

This mindset was in line with pre-election rhetoric too, where the success of independents and Greens was often presented as a 'theft' of seats that 'belonged' to the major parties. Josh Frydenberg accused his independent opponent Monique Ryan of being a 'fake independent' and 'part of [a] conspiracy to steal Liberal seats'. This was reported by Patricia Karvelas on ABC RN, and Karvelas leaned into that line of questioning during an interview with Ryan. The ABC ran a headline as far back as 2019 saying 'Independents looking to steal Mallee, one of the Nationals' safest seats'. It was a line they ran again in early July, more than six weeks after the election, with a headline that said 'The Greens success at the federal election saw them steal votes from unlikely places.' Labor party candidate for Richmond, Justine Elliot, even complained on Twitter that 'Greens are trying to beat Labor in Labor seats, and stop Labor forming a majority government.'

The very nerve of them!

Nothing better summed up the measured intent with which Labor and the rest of the political class wanted to make voters ignore what happened on 21 May, however, than that address given by Labor National Secretary Paul Erickson to the Press Club. He wasted no time in setting the terms of the story Labor wanted to tell for the next three years, saying, 'I don't accept that we are in some new epoch or new era where everything is different.' It was such a galling assertion, so obviously flying in the face of reality, but it spoke to the battle that faced the crossbench. And it was a powerful tactic, too, presuming as fact the very outcome that was being debated. It also played perfectly to the mindset of the insider political reporters who were his audience, telling them that they were 'savvy' enough to see past the surface-level aberration to the continuity flowing beneath.

I don't want to take anything away from Labor's victory, let alone suggest that it lacked legitimacy, but let's be clear: the alleged continuity Erickson was claiming as self-evident was fatally disrupted by the result of the 2022 election. Labor barely won a majority of seats, and had a historically low primary vote (32.6 per cent); their two-party majority of 52.13 per cent was made up of 13 per cent of votes that came from a combination of Greens (10 per cent), independents (2.5 per cent) and other candidates' preferences. Meanwhile, the Liberals had been wiped out in their heartland, and while the Nationals may have held onto all their seats, their share of the vote dropped in some seats, leaving them vulnerable to independent challenges at the next election. By any measure we *were* in 'a new epoch'. But Erickson's comment made it clear that they were going to act as if nothing had changed and that all the power remained with them. Anthony Albanese had already announced during the campaign that Labor would not enter into an agreement with the crossbench should Labor not get a majority, and he doubled down on this approach once his majority was established. Even before the new parliament sat on 26 July, he announced that the staff allocation for the independents would be cut substantially, from four to one, while the Greens, despite their increased representation, would not be allocated any additional staff.

The move was dressed up as a minor administrative adjustment, but it was an out-and-out power play, under-lined by the fact that some independents and smaller parties were treated more generously than the 'teals'. So although the new government cut the allocation of parliamentary staffers for, ostensibly, all crossbenchers, in fact, Rebekha Sharkie in Mayo, Bob Katter in Kennedy and Helen Haines in Indi were given an extra staffer each. The same was true of the two One Nation senators in the upper house and independent – and crucial swing vote – Senator David Pocock. It led to the ridiculous situation of some independents seeking crowdfunding for extra staff. Zali Steggall told reporters, quite rightly, that 'We should not be having to self-fund for the minimum adequate resources to service our community', and that it was 'incredibly unfair to provide different resources to different independents'.

Erickson had said nothing had changed, but the new prime minister's action showed clearly that it had. To cut crossbench staff in this way was an open admission that Labor was going to make political life as difficult as they could for those they obviously saw as Opposition players. Even the excuse Albanese proffered – that it was 'unfair' that the crossbench had more staff than individual government backbenchers – underlined the nature of the unfairness he was denying existed. The government backbench had full access to the resources of the Labor Party, and there was simply no comparison with the situation of the crossbench or the independents and minor parties in the Senate. The prime minister's comment was disingenuous at best.

The moment was telling in another way. The usually unflappable Zali Steggall responded with a series of tweets in which she let her anger show. She wrote that '@AlboMP didn't mind the Xbench having staff to put up alternative policies & push for anti-corruption & climate & hold the Morrison Govt to account but feels differently now. We are seeing his true character: dismissive of our communities & arrogant. No different to Morrison [sic].' She copped a lot of criticism for saying this, with some genuinely aggrieved at the comparison with Scott Morrison. Twitter heavyweight Ronni Salt noted that 'Whoever's doing @zalisteggall's media/social media advising needs to pull their head in – and pull it in fast. Her aggressive, nasty, high-handed tone here is brand damaging.' Salt added that she – along with many activists – had spent years working towards the removal of Scott Morrison, that he was a 'corrupt, lying, vainglorious bastard of a PM' and that 'Nobody did, or will, come within cooee of him.' Steggall's claim that Albanese was as bad as Morrison was therefore 'highly insulting', contemptuous of their work, Salt tweeted. It was a reasonable point to make, but Steggall's high-handed tone, and the uncharacteristic flash of public anger, were minor concerns compared to the underlying tension that Albanese's power play had brought into the open.

The strength of the Voices Of movement – its essence – lay in communities, in the voices of the people, and those voices will need continued elevation in all the debates that unfold. The goal, then, must be to change the underlying norms of the game, including in parliament itself, so that the sort of grassroots reform that happened organically on 21 May 2022 can be built upon. Numbers on the floor of the house will always be important, but as much as possible you want what is voted on to have arisen from meaningful deliberation, not just a set of options imposed by virtue of those numbers. Albanese's power play with staff numbers was the first time the Voices Of methodology had come head-to-head with the raw power of political numbers, and it exposed some fault lines.

This means that there are some fundamental challenges – practical and philosophical – the independents will face, and the first of them is that having now entered parliament, they must recognise they are no longer just a local member. Their responsibilities extend to the entire country, and while it is essential to continue to represent the communities that voted for them, their duty necessarily reaches beyond that immediate obligation. In a democracy, members of parliament don't just represent the people who voted for them. They also represent those who *didn't* vote for them – something that has added salience in Australia, where everyone is obliged to vote, and participation is regularly high.

As a local member, then, you are not just a voice for your electorate – part of your role is to be a voice for all of us, and so you must bring your local community along with you when you need to do things that aren't necessarily in their immediate interests but may be in the interests of the country as a whole. This expanded idea of representation is deeply embedded in conservative political history and theory, and was most famously articulated by Edmund Burke, the Irish-born British politician (who was also an economist and philosopher). Burke served as a member of the House of Commons between 1766 and 1794, and in his address to the electors of Bristol in 1774, he argued:

> [P]arliament is a deliberative assembly of one
> nation, with one interest, that of the whole; where,
> not local purposes, not local prejudices, ought

to guide, but the general good, resulting from
the general reason of the whole. You choose a
member indeed; but when you have chosen him,
he is not member of Bristol, but he is a member of
parliament.

He spelled out what this meant for the role of a local
representative:

[I]t ought to be the happiness and glory of a
representative to live in the strictest union, the
closest correspondence, and the most unreserved
communication with his constituents. Their wishes
ought to have great weight with him; their opinion,
high respect; their business, unremitted attention.
It is his duty to sacrifice his repose, his pleasures,
his satisfactions, to theirs; and above all, ever, and
in all cases, to prefer their interest to his own.

There is a 'but' coming, and the emphasis is mine:

But his unbiassed opinion, his mature judgment,
his enlightened conscience, he ought not to sacrifice
to you, to any man, or to any set of men living …
Your representative owes you, not his industry only,
but his judgment; and he betrays, instead of serving
you, if he sacrifices it to your opinion.

In other words, it is inevitable that challenges will arise
that do not settle on some theoretical halfway point

between opposing sides. There is no 'centre' onto which you can safely alight. You must choose. In an interview I did with Zali Steggall not long after she was elected in 2019, I asked what centrism meant to her, suggesting that she had taken positions on some issues that I didn't think could be described as centrist at all. For instance, she wanted a higher target than Labor did on carbon emission reductions, which was not a centrist position. She had also said she saw herself as 'fiscally conservative but socially liberal', and I didn't think that by itself was centrist either: the two things don't just balance each other out. Was her idea of centrism, I wondered, more about a willingness to compromise and not just stick to an 'ideological' line for the sake of it? Or was it something else? Steggall responded:

> When I refer to myself as 'centrist', what I am referring to is reflecting the majority views of the Warringah electorate. So, I see the centre as being socially progressive (as evidenced by the community's views on same-sex marriage and climate change for example) but with a more moderate liberal economic perspective on financial policy. I support lower taxes and a simplification of the deduction system. I support lower business taxes for small and medium businesses. I understand centre view will and should change over time, and I intend to listen and represent the views as they change. I agree with your description that it is a willingness to compromise and not just

stick to an 'ideological' line, which is what both major parties do.

It's a fair answer, and most of the other Voices Of independents are on record expressing similar views. But it leaves the central tension Burke was talking about unresolved: what do you do when the good of the country, as you see it, depends on decisions in which your social progressivism and fiscal conservatism clash, as they most certainly will around climate change, for instance? What do you do when the greater good clashes with the local good, as it almost certainly will over taxes and education? What do you do when one of the tools that got you to parliament in the first place risks undermining the possibility of other independents getting into parliament, as the current campaign financing laws certainly do?

The example Steggall used – the community's views on same-sex marriage – was a perfect illustration of the hole in the reasoning of 'centrists' more generally. Had she run for election in these communities 20 years earlier, community opinion on same-sex marriage would have been quite different, and to represent those views faithfully, Steggall would need to have been anti–gay marriage. The fact that the views of the electorate changed over time on this issue was testimony to the fact that various people *refused to accept* the views of their communities; that through various forms of activism, protest, argument, and testimony – often against seemingly insurmountable odds and violent opposition – the LGBTIQ+ community managed to change minds to the extent that the 2017 plebiscite got almost a 70 per cent national 'yes' vote. The 'centrism' Steggall lauds was built on decades of division and argument, *as so-called centrist positions always are.*

The Voices Of methodology of kitchen table discussion, of listening and finding things in common, is a crucial tool in achieving this sort of outcome, so preemptively committing yourself to the 'majority views' of the community as they exist in a moment in time forecloses on precisely the possibility of change inherent in that methodology. It isn't enough, in other words, to say that you will faithfully represent the views of your electorate. Representatives have a role in *shaping* those views, and this is what Burke was getting at when he said 'Your representative owes you, not his industry only, but his judgment.'

Okay, so hold all that in your mind while we dig in from another important angle.

The progressivism of the independents, of the Greens, and even of elements within Labor, emerged from a class of people attached to practical problem-solving. Guy Rundle and others are right to see this through the lens of knowledge-class politics, a class grounded in the tech industries of the 21st century. In an essay in *Meanjin*, he argued that the 'spread of a new value system, which I'm calling the "new progressivism", is largely due to the steady rise and sudden mass power of a relatively separate new social class: the knowledge class.' He writes:

Although it is a segment of traditional capitalist classes, it also has separate modes of accumulation and world construction. [It] has arisen from the growth of a knowledge/information economy in the West, at the same time as the industrial economy has declined – which accounts for its rapid increase in social power. The credo of the new progressivism is one of universalism, radical equality, transgression of given boundaries (of a certain type) and rejection of the contingent authority of tradition … This is neither some autonomous ethical upsurge, nor sinister brainwashing conspiracy. It is a class simply expressing the values its members find to be 'natural' and 'unquestionable' – values that were once marginal and avant-garde.

I would further argue that this knowledge class, perhaps paradoxically, sees itself as based in practice over theory, and that this mindset not only tends to override people's cynicism about politics more generally – politics as embodied in the do-nothing, blame-others approach of Scott Morrison that voters rejected on 21 May – it taps into a deep vein of Australian national identity as no-nonsense, practical, problem-solving people. We can illustrate the importance of this approach by looking at a key point in the 2022 election, when, in the final weeks of the campaign, it became apparent that those suffering a late diagnosis of Covid had missed the cut-off date for postal votes. This meant that potentially thousands of people would be disenfranchised: a Covid diagnosis meant they couldn't attend a polling booth on election day; the postal vote cut-off date meant they could not vote by post. As this situation became apparent, neither major party, nor the Australian Electoral Commission, seemed particularly concerned, even when Twitter lit up with complaints.

Responding in real time, the independent candidate for Kooyong, Dr Monique Ryan, announced she would mount a court challenge against the cut-off date, and she called for donations with which to fund the action. She was looking for $60K, but only a few hours after the fundraising website was launched on the night of Thursday 19 May, she had raised $73K. The next day, her lawyers lodged an application in the Federal Court against the AEC cut-off date, and then, recognising the damage the case would cause his government, Scott Morrison stepped in (not up) and changed the regulations, allowing Covid-affected people to vote by phone.

It was a perfect example of how a motivated outsider could achieve things the mainstream brushed aside, and how can-do problem-solving could trump the complacency of a self-serving status quo. Ryan made the point that it was 'extraordinary that we had to crowdfund last night to sue our own government for the ability to vote. This was entirely predictable. Who caused this situation? Scott Morrison. Who provided certainty? An Independent.' Ryan's success with this action rippled across social media and may have pushed some voters over the line towards the independents – voters who, not without justification, had been wondering up until that point if it was worth risking their vote on an unknown political entity.

I am suggesting that people welcomed evidence of politicians achieving some goal, just as they did during the early period of the Covid pandemic, and that this will be an ongoing aspect of the success of independents. The loss of state capacity that had occurred over the 40 years of the neoliberal experiment – the ability to raise taxes and do things on behalf of citizens, including seeing to it that they could vote – had left communities bereft, precisely because neoliberalism solves for the individual and not the community. As the kitchen table approach moved us back towards that practice of collective action, the independents could be seen as part of a project of rebuilding state capacity, and the role of the current 'three-party' parliament will be to translate local move-ments into practical, problem-solving governance at the federal level. As the Grattan Institute wrote in the lead-up to the election, 'The new federal government should adopt a framework that weighs both the value of each reform and its practical "doability". It should give highest priority to the reforms that are of high value and can be feasibly achieved by the federal government.'

Amen, but not just the new federal government: this practical approach should be pursued by all members of parliament.

Still, we need to be careful not to take explanations such as 'the knowledge class' too far, in part because the evidence on the ground suggests that the power of personal engagement overrides such identifications, and they may themselves be part of a two-party mindset and miss what we might call third-party reasoning. Part of the transformation we are seeing in Australian politics – and the reason we can safely say that a 'third force' is here to stay – is that the Voices Of methodology suggests voters are no longer wedded to the idea that only the two major parties can deliver the things they want from a government.

Greens activist Joanna Horton, writing on the *Green Agenda* website, described her experience door-knocking for the party in Brisbane as illustrative of this point. She found that people were far less willing to accept the 'party of government' arguments Labor was using in the area as a reason to stick with the 'majors', and rejected the idea that the only way 'to make legislative change [was] through holding a parliamentary majority, as opposed to a "protest party" like the Greens'. She said that failing to appreciate this change 'represents a fatal misreading of what the average voter cares about in terms of politics', and that most of the people she spoke with 'were not at all swayed by the idea of voting for a "party of government".' She wrote that there was 'an understanding of politics as [aspirational], that it's acceptable or even useful to have a big, bold policy agenda that stands for some broader political vision to work towards.' Therefore:

> [A]nalyses seeking to slot voters into demographic groups (e.g. 'knowledge class', or 'latte-sippers') are necessary, to some extent, for the purpose of making

large-scale arguments about voting behaviour. However, it would be a mistake to transfer that logic to ground campaigning. The Greens' success in Queensland came not from targeted mailouts, robocalls, or text messages, but from having tens of thousands of *individual* conversations, which were often rich and surprising. We never assumed the role of experts there to convince voters of our policies. Rather, we took the position that we had a lot to learn from the people we spoke to. In this way, the ground campaigning effort was valuable in not only bringing voters over to the Greens, but also in better aligning the party's policies and messaging with what voters cared about.

The challenge now facing the 'teals', the Greens, and what I think will be an increasing number of new candidates from this knowledge-class formation after the *next* election is how they might extend the benefits of the political renewal they have enjoyed in their wealthier electorates to the country more generally. A truly progressive nation, one in which there was a levelling up beyond what has been possible over the last 40 years of neoliberalism, would be one in which the sort of change that has happened in the deep blue electorates (and some red ones) was able to happen across the country.

The risk is that we fall back on the inevitable conservatism of the status quo, even if it is an altered status quo, and opt for stability over justice; for stasis over dynamism. That the independents' movement coalesces into a new party of social liberalism and assumes the role the Liberal Party itself once played. That would not be progress, let alone progressive.

Another risk is that Clive Palmer, or some other deep pocket from the deep right, will take note of the kitchen table methodology and use it for their own purposes. Fortunately, I think the chances of this are slim – Palmer's position on the political spectrum is simply too authoritarian to engage in the bottom-up, listening-to methodology – but it is possible some scam version of it will arise that could get the job done, for at least one electoral cycle. In fact, evidence of this scam approach emerged in the lead-up to the Victorian state election as Liberal Party operatives revealed that they had been training candidates to run as 'independents' in marginal Labor seats. 'Labor will not go unmolested by independents in their own seats,' a high-ranking Liberal official told reporters at *The Age*. This is precisely the sort of corruption of the Voices Of approach we should expect to see more of as the Liberal Party, in particular, tries to claw back the ground it has lost.

The grassroots engagement we have seen over the last few years is vitally important to a progressive nation, as is the recognition by the independents that their expanded role in the political life of the nation might put national goals in conflict with local ones. But political power is about giving substance to change, so let's run through some ideas of what those areas of change might involve. In so doing, I don't want to make a laundry list of all the policies I think should be pursued – it would be long! – but to concentrate on those that can transform the structures of our democratic institutions so that co-operation and discussion are installed as the standard operating procedure.

Arguably the most urgent of all such reforms was raised by author and commentator Jane Gilmore in the immediate aftermath of the election, in a piece she wrote for my *Future of Everything* newsletter. Gilmore had tried to run as an independent Senate candidate at the 2022 election but found herself up against barriers to participation that many prospective independents face, not least finding the money to enable her to compete against the major parties or other candidates with deeper pockets than hers. She wrote:

> I started far too late – in January this year – and four months is not nearly long enough to jump through all the bureaucratic hoops deliberately designed to prevent new, Independent candidates entering parliament. Even if I'd had a year, I didn't have the connections, staff, infrastructure, experience, or knowledge – or the money it takes to buy those things – that I needed to get a campaign off the ground. With three years to plan for the next election, I might be able to do it. Might. But if there is no effective reform to campaign finance, no amount of time will be enough for me, or any other new Independent, to run a successful bid against the million-dollar candidates selected by large donors.

Gilmore noted that campaign finance reform was not something an Integrity Commission would necessarily deal with, so it needed its own champions, and chief among these should be the independents themselves. As former Liberal Party Treasurer Michael Yabsley wrote in *Crikey*, the 'major parties will never take this cause on without external pressure. It's a gravy train that suits both sides of politics and most other political players as well.' He argued that 'complete reform of this broken system is required,' and he suggested those reforms should include 'real-time disclosure' of donations, as well as limits on the amount of money given. His key point was that 'the problem is ... not how much and when it is given, but the fact that it is given at all.' In a post-election edition of *Four Corners*, he said, 'the truth is that most politicians get their hands dirty with fundraising', while in the *Crikey* article, he highlighted the role played by Simon Holmes à Court's Climate 200 group, which he saw as a surprisingly benign player under the circumstances, saying the 'problem for Climate 200 is that it risks catching the big party virus of relying on big money'. Gilmore made a similar point, arguing that, in 2022, we got lucky:

> Holmes à Court supported smart women with conviction and integrity, while Clive Palmer splattered millions of dollars over Queensland and the entire internet to no effect. But if Palmer (or others like him) were taking notes over the last six weeks, we might get a very different result next time.

The key logic of any reform, Yabsley has argued, should be 'to strike at the root of the problem' by mandating 'low-value, high-volume fundraising', and he has developed a ten-point plan to achieve just that (via *Crikey*):

- A $200 cap on political donations per individual, covering the entire electoral cycle in each jurisdiction
- A cap on election expenditure, including advertising
- Only enrolled Australian citizens permitted to make donations
- All donations to be anonymous and non-disclosable, as their small size would remove the case for disclosure
- No other entities, corporations, unions, or organisations to be permitted to make donations
- All public funding of elections to be removed
- Laws to be enforced with criminal sanctions carrying custodial sentences, including targeting the aggregation of small donations into significantly larger donations
- National uniform donation laws across all states and territories
- Electoral commissions to police laws and review caps
- A bespoke federal/state body to develop a program of election debates and set media pieces during election campaigns.

There was some evidence the new government was cognisant of the need for such reforms, and the Special Minister for State, Don Farrell, has said that, before the next election, Labor will introduce legislation that will, among other things, place a lower cap on campaign donations, which is currently set at $10K. I asked Gilmore about the government's plans and she told me she thought it was likely nothing more than 'bait and switch' and said that 'I think it's very unlikely to happen. Everyone has a vested interest in maintaining the status quo.' Certainly, the Liberal Party has made clear they will not support any reform, with the federal director of the party, Andrew Hirst, saying, 'the Liberal party does not support changes to these arrangements that would unnecessarily add to the already considerable administrative and compliance burdens placed on political parties.' The Greens, on the other hand, have a suite of reform options, and they include a $1000 donation cap as well as new rules around transparency, and increased penalties for failure to comply with the new rules.

Kylea Tink, the independent MP for North Sydney, told the *Guardian* that she supported 'greater transparency' around political donations and said caps were 'a good idea', but suggested that 'the tricky part in this will be coming to what that number needs to look like.' She went so far as to suggest that issues around real-time disclosure of donations, along with truth in political advertising, were bigger issues than the size of donations, which bears out Gilmore's concern about whether the political will for deep reform exists. Tink said that 'without the backing of a party the need to be able to invest to build name recognition and the agenda I was running on was absolutely essential' – a comment that speaks to the reluctance to interfere with the Climate 200 type of organisation.

There is another way in which campaign finance reform would be 'good politics'.

Already, sections of the political right are running the criticism that the Voices Of independents are self-interested, privileged dilettantes, and that their signature issue of climate change is a 'luxury' issue. Writing in the *Spectator*, for instance, Rebecca Weiser said, 'Green and teal rent-seeking elites have been helped immeasurably by an education system that indoctrinates children and young adults, from kindergarten through to university, in the cult of climate catastrophism', and that 'Teal climate policies are trophies for rich women, diamond necklaces to flaunt at harbourside parties. They are not signs of virtue; they are vanities.'

This is a nonsense argument, attempting to reignite the 'elites versus ordinary people' tactics of the 1990s, but it will persist, and may have some traction, as sections of the media latch onto it over the next three years. The best way to kill it dead would be to embrace campaign finance reform in such a way as to guarantee that the poorer suburbs could participate in the democratic process on the same playing field as the 'teals', thus undermining any claims of elitism.

The bottom line is that campaign financing of the sort engaged in by Climate 200 is at loggerheads with the kitchen table, grassroots approach to democracy that defines the Voices Of movement. It is part of the same process of donations by vested interests – from the mining sector to the gambling industry – that are a key factor undermining good governance in the name of those interests. Campaign finance reform of the sort put forward by Michael Yabsley is the only way of breaking this nexus between big money donors and politics, and the essentially benign (even positive) nature of Climate 200 doesn't cancel out this sort of state capture – it merely normalises it. Campaign finance reform is therefore a key test of crossbench integrity and their commitment to bottom-up democratic practice.

Campaign finance reform goes hand in hand with another important reform: the way in which we vote. While we can accept the efficacy – even the beauty – of the preferential system that Australia uses in the lower house, we should not close our minds to the fact that something better might be possible. If, as a nation, we really have moved beyond the two-party system; if we want a more diverse and fully representative selection of politicians in parliament; if we want to fully realise the benefits of the grassroots, kitchen table campaigning conducted by the Voices Of organisations around the country, then it makes sense to consider the possibility of adopting an electoral system that enhances all those characteristics. And that means considering proportional representation (PR) for the lower house.

A full analysis of the exact PR system Australia could use is beyond the scope of this discussion, but we can at least talk about the underlying principles and advantages. The key idea behind PR is that it allows for multi-member electorates, with seats distributed on the basis of the proportion of votes won, whether those candidates are members of a party or have run as independents. Political scientists measure this ratio with a system called the Gallagher index, where the lower the number assigned by the index to an election outcome, the more accurately that result balances votes with seats.

Under Australia's preferential voting system, we regularly receive a Gallagher index score of between 8 and 12, which is quite high – that is, disproportional. It means that some parties in our system are getting more seats than their raw vote suggests they should, while others are getting fewer. New Zealand, for instance, which uses a mixed-member system of proportional representation, typically scores around 5 on the Gallagher index. At the 2022 election, Australia's score blew out to 16.5, which means that in the current parliament, Labor has received a disproportionately high number of seats relative to their vote, while the Greens have received far fewer seats than their vote would allow in a more proportional system. As analyst Ben Raue has argued on his *Tally Room* website, while it is 'clear a majority preferred a Labor government, I'm just not sure they voted for a Labor majority'.

Again, in saying all this, I am not casting doubt on the legitimacy of the 2022 election result, or even on the fact that Labor has formed government on their own, and nor was Raue. In fact, Raue's way of expressing this is that 'while I don't think Australians have expressed a clear view about the desirability of a majority Labor government, they have clearly expressed a preference for a Labor-led government over a Coalition-led government.' If that is correct, and I think it is, then it suggests very strongly the need for electoral reform that can better enable the possibility of minority government.

There is no doubt that Australians distributed their preferences in accordance with exactly that – their preferences for certain candidates/parties – and that traditionally they have voted strategically, recognising that the system might not deliver their first preference a seat in the parliament, and that this strategic approach was accentuated at the 2022 election. Typically, Greens voters know that their party will not form government, but they will give their first preference to the Greens and second to Labor. In seats where the contest is close between Labor and the Greens – something that is becoming more common in certain metropolitan seats, such as Macnamara in Melbourne – more people are willing to vote 1 for the Greens if they see them as having a chance of taking the seat (and at the 2022 election, Greens candidate Steph Hodgins-May was less than 2000 votes from winning on first preferences). As political analyst Grant Wyeth argued in *Diplomat Magazine*, Australians have been using the voting system to register their preferences outside the 'major' parties for decades now, and 2022 continued that trend, 'a lesson that is proving difficult for Australia's major parties – and those invested in them – to accept.' He makes the point that preferential voting gives a nuanced insight into what voters want, and he explains the power of that system very well:

> In a number of well-targeted seats … independent candidates were able to bring the Liberal Party's candidates down to a primary vote of between 40 and 45 percent, which allowed an independent candidate to sweep up Labor and Greens preferences to win the seat. This was not achieved by 'rigging' the voting system, but by understanding how consensus is created through the system, and being aware that a majority of the public in that electorate preferred to not have a Liberal Party MP, even if they had different ideas about which candidate should replace them. Preferential voting created the democratic compromise in favour of the independent.

I want to be clear here (again): I am not suggesting there is anything illegitimate about Australia's election results. All I am saying is that we can do better, especially if we are going to take seriously the idea that our country is not neatly divided into a two-party system, something the 2022 election result clearly showed. I don't think we should have a voting system that allows only one of two parties (for the purposes of this discussion, I am presuming the Coalition is functionally a single party) to form government and provide a prime minister and then rule in a way that requires little further recourse to the rest of the representatives in the house. What I am saying is that voting trends – and the 2022 election in particular – indicated that Australians were keen to break out of the two-party system; that they were using all the electoral tools available to them to do just that; and that therefore there is a strong case that our elected representatives should take our concerns, as expressed through our voting patterns, seriously and reform the system so that it is more proportional.

As I have already noted, it was very discouraging to hear the Labor national secretary say at the Press Club that he didn't accept that 'we are in some new epoch or new era where everything is different', but of course, he would say that. And that is precisely why we need institutional reform, so that the whims of a given party are constrained in the interests of everybody else. Labor's national secretary doesn't get to define reality.

The biggest risk people raise with PR is the danger of allocating seats to minor parties in a way that undermines the stability of government, as a gaggle of small parties and independents make demands and set conditions so that the government is consistently threatened with withdrawal of support and therefore collapses. It is a reasonable concern, but it is easily answered, not just by the fact that Australia has a long history of making electoral innovation work – from the secret ballot to compulsory voting – but by the fact that there is considerable research suggesting you can design a system of PR that meets the requirements of diversity (fairly distributing seats on the basis of votes won) while avoiding the excesses of too many smaller parties creating instability.

Political scientists John Carey and Simon Hix, for example, examined PR systems across 81 countries and concluded that the key to the design of a stable-but-representative system was the idea of 'district magnitude', which is the number of seats available in each electoral district. Under non-PR systems – such as preferential voting and first-past-the-post voting systems – each electoral district (what we in Australia would call an electorate) provides a single member to parliament. Under PR, electorates can provide more than one representative to parliament, based on the proportion of votes received. The number of members a single seat can provide is a key element of the design of a PR system, ranging from what Carey and Hix call a high-magnitude approach – where a larger number of candidates in each electorate is eligible to sit in the parliament – to a low-magnitude approach, where fewer candidates are eligible. Carey and Hix argue that the 'sweet spot' occurs in low-magnitude proportional electoral systems:

> Consistent with the traditional view of electoral systems in political science, we find that single-member district systems tend to produce a small number of parties and single-party government, but also have relatively unrepresentative parliaments. On the other side, electoral systems with large multi-member districts have highly representative parliaments, but also have highly fragmented

party systems and unwieldy multi-party coalition governments. In contrast, electoral systems with small multi-member districts – with median magnitude between four and eight seats, for example – tend to have highly representative parliaments and a moderate number of parties in parliament and in government.

Stability *and* a more representative parliament.

As another political scientist, Arend Lijphart, has noted, 'the beauty of PR is that, in addition to producing proportionality and minority representation, it treats all groups – ethnic, racial, religious, or even noncommunal groups – in a completely equal and even-handed fashion. Why deviate from full PR at all?'

Why, indeed?

As I say, the full discussion of the pros and cons of designing the system is beyond the scope of this book, but it is important to recognise that it is possible to design a system of PR that balances electoral proportionality against parliamentary stability – New Zealand providing the most obvious example – and I find it hard to conceive of compelling democratic reasons for persisting with a system that doesn't deliver as close a match as possible between how people vote and how those votes are represented in parliament. A crossbench that took the logic of their own rhetoric of fair representation seriously cannot avoid engaging with this sort of electoral reform: it speaks to the very essence of the sort of democracy they represent.

Another reform the new parliament needs to consider is sortition. To achieve a system of government that properly takes account of citizens' views and allows as many people as possible to deliberate on democratic outcomes, we must make room for non-elected citizens to be part of the process, and sortition – random selection as opposed to voting – enables this. 'Citizens juries', 'community assemblies', 'deliberative polls', and other such gatherings, made up of citizens chosen at random from a representative selection of the community (as we do with juries) are brought together to learn about and discuss specific policy matters. The guiding principle of such gatherings is that they are flexible enough to allow people to develop trust and ways of working together, but solid enough to allow us to '[build] institutional structures around the behaviours and norms we develop in practice, [to] forge the path from community projects to transformative, systemic change', as Tim Hollo writes in his book, *Living Democracy*.

I have written about this idea more extensively in *The Future of Everything*, and there are plenty of other studies – but it is worth noting that citizen assemblies can be designed as either a permanent feature of the apparatus of government, or as periodically convened gatherings designed to let citizens adjudicate on specific matters of policy or issues of community concern. In other words, there is a maximalist and a minimalist approach.

An example of a permanent form of citizen assembly exists in Ostbelgien, the German-speaking region of

Belgium with a population of 77 000. Their parliament, the Deutschsprachige Gemeinschaft Belgien, which sits in Eupen, has included since 2019 two assemblies constituted by sortition. There is a permanent 'Citizens council' (Bürgerrat) consisting of 24 citizens who serve for 18 months. The role of the council is to select topics and set the agenda for 'citizen assemblies' (Bürgerversammlungen). There is a maximum of three of these assemblies each year and their members are also chosen by sortition, with consideration given to age, gender and education quotas. These assemblies produce recommendations to the German-speaking parliament, and the parliament is obliged to discuss the proposals that come from the Bürgerversammlungen. They can accept or reject recommendations from the assemblies, but they must provide a justification for the decision, whatever they decide.

In Australia, economist Nicholas Gruen has been a key figure in arguing for some form of people's chamber based on sortition, and, like me, he sees the transformation of the 2022 election as a key moment for instituting such reform in Australia. He has written that 'sortition or selection by lot offers a powerful bulwark against the power of elites and interest groups', as well as – or simply *by* – 'allowing face-to-face deliberation amongst citizens in an environment in which their relative power is equalised'.

In arguing for sortition, I am not saying that voting is bad. But I am saying that it is not enough. We need at least one institution, perhaps one of the houses of parliament (maximalist), or some auxiliary to those houses (minimalist), where ordinary people get to represent themselves and participate in the governing process. We need, in other words, to institutionalise the kitchen table methodology. Such an approach to governance can seem radical because we have allowed voting alone to become synonymous with democracy, forgetting there is more to self-government (democracy) than showing up at the ballot box every three or four years. We have lost that sense of ongoing self-rule that is the heart of democracy, as well as the sense that participation can itself be a source of joy and empowerment.

Majority rule is an important tool of democratic decision making and we need it. But democracy is not majority rule; it is self-rule. Majority rule only has legitimacy if the interests of the minority are also acknowledged, heeded and protected. Nobody gets everything they want, but everybody gets a say, and the genius of the Voices Of methodology is precisely what Mary Crooks from Victorian Women's Trust articulated: 'Everybody who participated – everybody – needs to have a sense that what they said and what their group said has actually been taken into account.' A democracy cannot function properly unless there are institutions and practices that allow all of us to exercise our ability to have a say in the way the country is organised. You cannot reduce political participation to the act of voting alone. You cannot reduce the role of the citizen to the limited ability to choose from the array of insiders on offer. You must provide ways for citizens to participate in governance without electing them to anything, and citizens' assemblies based on sortition are the best way of achieving this. As I've noted, such gatherings bring together expert and lay opinion in deliberative forums that allow informed outcomes to emerge based on the principle of experts for means, citizens for ends, and they thus go a long way towards meaningfully dissolving divides between elites and ordinary citizens, or between insiders and outsiders.

To put it another way, democracy can accommodate stratification across various social formations. The idea that there are specialists, intellectuals, technocrats and other types of expert who may be rewarded (socially and monetarily) more than those with more quotidian skills is not necessarily damaging to the idea of democracy as self-rule. If the overarching system allows the benefits of specialisation to filter through adequately to the population, it can maintain democratic legitimacy. What democracy *cannot* accommodate is a culture of insiders and outsiders. You cannot have a culture of participants and observers and maintain legitimacy, because democratic legitimacy is arrived at through participation – something that was at the heart of the Voices Of methodology. And it is not as if we don't already allow such gatherings, or that we don't understand the positive effect they can have. Australia, at various levels of government, has used citizens' assemblies – I have witnessed several of them – and it is extraordinary, the powerful democratic effect they have on participants. I noted in an article for the *Griffith Review* how transformative the experience can be, and gave the example of a participant in the deliberative poll held in Canberra in 1999 on the question of Australia becoming a republic: 'Can I just say that as an elder citizen that I've been tremendously informed and stimulated by this gathering. I would just like to say how wonderfully I've seen the democratic process at work.'

The *Guardian*, reporting on the 2017 citizens' assembly in Ireland that led to a referendum on abortion rights, noted that 'Assembly participants certainly seem delighted to have taken part. Of more than half a dozen consulted … all were hugely positive.' Liz Connell Jones, a 63-year-old retired teacher and mother of two from Wexford, south-east Ireland, was quoted as saying, 'I'm almost sad it's coming to an end. It's been a life-changing experience for me.'

The Voices Of movement has restored our commitment to such participation, but if we are going to reap the benefits of what has been set in motion, we need to institutionalise the processes that achieved them. We must do everything we can – from campaign finance reform to electoral reform, and sortition – to make sure the change that is under way is not only sustained but continues to head in a democratic direction. I recognise the challenge involved in all this, but I think the Voices Of independents who emerged in the lead-up to the 2022 election have a particular obligation to take these further reforms seriously. What's more, their own example shows exactly what can be achieved if we refuse to put such reforms in the too-hard basket.

Politics will remain messy and forever involve trade-offs. Circles can't be squared. What matters is that you have the tools in place that allow people to agree on what irregular form the final square/circle will take. Civilisation is the ability to abide by the resulting imperfection. And then we strive for a more perfect squared circle.

The easy bit in politics is choosing between right and wrong. It is much harder to choose between outcomes that are equally good, and what is good for Wentworth is not necessarily good for Corangamite. What is good for someone on $200K per year is not necessarily good for someone on a tenth of that. What is good for the landlord clashes with what is good for the tenant. In the end, local representatives are always faced with the possibility of the local good clashing with the national good, and having to decide whether you simply go along with the views of your electorate, or whether, like Edmund Burke, you undertake to bring people around to the national view. It is not an impossible hurdle, but it is one that the new independents need to think about deeply. And the key to addressing these issues in the most fruitful manner is to bring the co-operative, listening approach of the Voices Of movement to the bigger arena of the federal parliament itself.

The question the independent candidates will have to ask themselves, therefore, is whether they will be agents of change who use their skills and momentum to bring what they have achieved in their electorates to the rest of the country – to those electorates without the advantages of the ones they represent – or whether will they settle, pulling up the ladder behind them. It is one thing to style yourself as a centrist – as they all do – but, policy by policy, you must take a position, and if they are going to be true to their commitment to take expert advice, as well as be open to what their communities want, centrism is not going to be enough. I am very hopeful they will rise to the challenge, and am encouraged by comments like those from Dr Monique Ryan, who has defined her independence in these terms:

> I am not a one-dimensional political creature.
> I like aspects of each party's platform, support some
> policies and disagree with others, applaud some
> gestures and abhor others. To think any person
> can fit neatly in a political box is to misunderstand
> and underestimate human nature. Like many
> Australians I have had moments of affinity with
> different parties, but voting with your values means
> deciding on the issues at each election and not
> being tied to blue, red or green.

This is a useful approach, but it needs to go further. It is not simply a matter of choosing between parties or ideologies, or even between good and bad policy: as I've said, sometimes it is about choosing between conflicting good policies, and under such circumstances, falling back on 'I will do what my community wants' is not going to solve the problem. What your community wants may clash with what the country needs.

There was much excitement about the passing of Labor's legislation for a 43 per cent carbon target in the first two weeks of the new parliament, but when Zali Steggall declared in that moment that 'The climate wars are nearly over', we saw the limits of co-operation and compromise. Given that the legislation itself didn't require more of the government than that they report to parliament every year on what progress had been made towards an emissions reduction target, with no enforcement mechanism, it was hard to see what the excitement was about. You couldn't help but feel that performative co-operation was being elevated over addressing the actual problems of climate change.

The closer we come to a genuinely powerful crossbench, one that has the numbers to make a difference in votes on the floor of the house, the more we need to embed the Voices Of methodology of listening and deliberation into the institution of parliament itself in a way that leads to genuine change. This is the immense challenge that faces the new crossbench, the new third power of Australian politics, and again, there is reason to be hopeful. A close look at the way in which the Voices Of movement has developed shows that the organisers and candidates have been on a steep learning curve: such was the nature of being outsiders. But at every point, they have risen to the challenge and managed to forge a worthwhile response. They have remained flexible enough to keep learning, and that will be the challenge as they work within the halls of power amidst the pull of the automatic stabilisers trying to resist the change they represent and embody.

The important question of this moment, then, is not whether the Liberal Party can find their way back to electability, or what primary vote Labor might get next time. It isn't even whether the independents who found their way to power via a methodology of listening and learning can keep doing that, now that they have some power of their own. It is about whether this greater reform is possible. It is a huge task, and we must be careful not to load unrealistic expectations onto a crossbench that still doesn't have the numbers in parliament, and that, like any political formation, will have to deal with all the things that can go wrong. So much depends upon a teal wheelbarrow, and we can't expect it to carry all our hopes and dreams of political renewal. Instead, we all must work to entrench the Voices Of methodology of grassroots democracy, so that our system of governance is truly transformed.

Conclusion

Raising the voices of us

Asking yourself a question, that's how resistance begins.
And then ask that very question to someone else.

Remco Campert

On 21 May 2022, Tanya and I stood in a line outside our local polling booth at the Victorian College of Arts Secondary School (VCASS) in Southbank in Melbourne, a school our son had attended from Year 9 until Year 12, and it was a beautiful sunny day, maybe 17 degrees, the inner city air crisp, with the sense of being balanced precisely on the edge of a change of season. A season of change.

Around 50 others were lined up with us, and there was a buzz in the air. People chatted with each other, and with the workers representing the various parties and independents, and everyone was calm and polite, even those from the United Australia Party. It is compulsory in our country to enrol to vote, but no-one in this queue was there under sufferance. People may have been fitting the task in between shopping and lunch, or between weekend sports and dinner, or a show at the nearby Malthouse Theatre, but there was no sense at all that they resented this mild democratic obligation. How different it all seemed from the image portrayed in the media of an angry, divided nation disengaged from politics.

We weren't that. Not in the way they meant.

And at this election, least of all.

What we were disengaged from, I realised on that glorious day – with more certainty than I generally allow – was the political class itself: the politicians and the media, the journalists and the commentators, the business leaders and all the other insiders who wield power in our island nation. We were disengaged from the mindless media coverage of the election, which, during the previous six weeks, had descended into farce, dominated as it was by performative journalists looking to trip up the Leader of the Opposition to feed their narrative that he was unprepared for office and gaffe-prone. We had little interest in a governing class that didn't govern and instead produced images of themselves doing things they thought played well on social and traditional media. We were well and truly over the usual boxes the political class put us into, particularly those labelled 'Labor' and 'Liberal'.

After maybe 20 minutes, the queue winding through the corridors of VCASS reached the theatre area, the arena where my son had trained as part of the school's dance program, and I felt like doing a little dance myself. I had my name crossed off the roll, was handed my green ballot paper for the lower house and the flapping white sheet for the Senate, and took myself to one of the cardboard booths and did my democratic duty. I popped my folded papers into their boxes, thanked the AEC people who were gently ushering us around, and walked home with Tanya and had some lunch. When the polls closed at six o'clock, we headed to a friend's place to watch coverage of the count.

The government changed and the country changed. And it also stayed the same.

It took about two minutes for the grind of politics-as-usual to reinstate itself, and even as it became apparent Labor would form government, Leigh Sales, hosting the ABC's coverage, asked her guest, Labor's Tanya Plibersek, 'What has Labor done wrong?'. Once sworn in, the new prime minister, Anthony Albanese, set about fulfilling travel obligations committed to by the previous government, taking a number of overseas trips, and was immediately chastised by sections of the media for spending too much time outside the country. As floodwaters rose in Sydney (again) and the new prime minister met with the president of Ukraine during one of these trips, the Opposition and sections of the media compared his absence to that of Scott Morrison holidaying in Hawaii during the 2019 bushfires. The new Opposition leader, Peter Dutton, was installed unopposed by his party room, and as *Media Watch* host Paul Barry noted, 'The conservative head-kicker and new opposition leader [was] very busy ... getting everyone to tell us what a lovely guy he is.' Barry showed a dozen or so headlines and article extracts to illustrate the point: 'Dutton 2.0: I'll be a gentler and caring me' (*The Australian*, 26 May 2022).

The Murdoch media's transfer of allegiance to the new Liberal leader was as seamless as a British coronation: the king was dead, long live the king, and we were straight back into the narratives and frameworks and reality creation that the election result suggested most people had rejected. Even the new government fell into old habits, and despite repeated assurances they would be co-operative and consultative, they started speaking of mandates, as if a primary vote of less than 33 per cent could give them any such thing. As if you could assert a mandate *and* be co-operative. They not only lopped the staffing allocation to the crossbench, they succumbed to the culture war games the media delighted in, buckling on matters to do with abortion and trans rights. In her daily column in *The Monthly*, Rachel Withers asked, quite rightly, 'If Labor can't stand up for women's and trans rights now, so soon after an election win that was a clear repudiation of sexism and transphobia (among other things), when can it?'

Labor also started relitigating the 2009 decision by the Greens to vote down Kevin Rudd's Carbon Pollution Reduction Scheme (CPRS), and it was déjà vu all over again. This policy decision had been a point of contention among Labor and Greens voters since it happened and was regularly alluded to, with Labor using it as a stick to beat the Greens with at every opportunity, arguing that it showed they weren't 'serious' about reform and had indulged in small party grandstanding to the detriment of the country. The Greens countered with the perfectly reasonable point that Rudd's policy was not adequate to the task it purportedly addressed, and that it potentially made things worse. Climate expert and activist Ketan Joshi wrote on the *Renew Economy* website that 'The CPRS was objectively a terrible piece of policy; a litany of dodgy international offsets and fossil subsidies blended with greenwashing and ultra-weak targets, the result of aggressive lobbying from the fossil fuel industry.' Many on the Labor side conceded as much, *sotto voce*, but relied on an argument that said that whatever the CPRS's failings, it was a start, better than nothing, and the Greens were wrong to miss the chance to do *something*. Journalist Katharine Murphy ran a similar line just before the new parliament first sat, writing in the *Guardian* that 'the new Albanese government, the teal buffer state and the Greens have to decide what's most important: is it taking the critical first step to end the climate wars, or is it preserving their political product differentiation at voter expense?'

Whatever you think of the pros and cons of the central case, it was clear Labor resurrected the dispute in this moment as another power play to help justify sticking to a carbon target that everyone from climate experts to the South Pacific nations to the independents on the crossbench were telling them was inadequate. To suggest, as Murphy had, that rejecting Labor's approach was 'product differentiation' was insulting to those who simply had a different view, and yet another example of how even the best journalists can be captured by the outdated frames of political competition, even as they were calling for people to compromise. And while it is easy to sympathise with Labor's dilemma of not wanting to renege on an election commitment – knowing full well the media would tip a bucket on them – how ridiculous was it that they, and the media, would rather honour a promise to a flawed policy than negotiate with other members of parliament for a better outcome?

Could there be a clearer illustration of how counter-productive our politics can be?

You couldn't help but feel let down. We had just participated in one of the most extraordinary elections of the last 50 years, had achieved the sort of democratic renewal that was eluding nearly every other country on earth, and it was like none of it mattered. The media, the mainstream politicians, business – all the pillars of the status quo – picked up where they had left off and even the new boss, as Zali Steggall had said when Labor cut the staffing allocation for the crossbench, was behaving like the old boss. It felt like the final lines of *Animal Farm*: 'The creatures outside looked from pig to man, and from man to pig, and from pig to man again; but already it was impossible to say which was which.' It was all so stupid and short-sighted. By the time the new parliament sat for the first time on 26 July, it was obvious that Labor, the media and the official Opposition were set to conduct themselves according to the mindset of the two-party system that Australians had rejected with more force than they ever had in their history.

So where did this leave the independents and the

change they had instigated and represented, let alone us, the voters?

The 2022 election showed that we were still a country that saw a role for government, that we valued community, and we expected government to help manage the risks that any community faces, including matters to do with healthcare, aged care and disaster relief. No-one thought a GoFundMe campaign organised by a federal minister was an acceptable way to respond to a regional emergency. But the election also showed that the years of neoliberalism had changed us more than is often acknowledged, and the rise of independents at the expense of the former major parties was a sign of this. We were settling on a more overt form of individuality than had previously been the case, the traditional ties of party loyalty dissolving, and their promise of stability and she'll-be-right reassurance no longer holding sway. This was perhaps most apparent in the way in which governments and communities responded to the ongoing Covid pandemic, the way it which it had become difficult to reintroduce public health measures such as mask wearing that all health authorities said would help control the spread of the disease and keep us all safer. Honorary Professor Stephen Duckett from the School of Population and Global Health at the University of Melbourne noted that Scott Morrison's hands-off approach to managing Covid had 'weakened the states' social licence to pursue effective public health measures'. Writing in *The Conversation*, he argued:

Despite the much-vaunted national cabinet, for most of 2020 and 2021 there was no coherent national leadership of COVID-19 response. Then-Prime Minister Scott Morrison and other federal ministers downplayed COVID risks and undermined state public health measures. They attacked lockdowns, state border closures and school shutdowns, while dog-whistling to anti-vaxxers.

We were also less inclined to be led by journalists' versions of events, by the way in which they framed issues, and the fact that people could gather on social media and reach their own conclusions was a change in momentum that the status quo was ill-equipped to deal with. The often pearl-clutching terror with which it reacted to things that happened 'online' showed how unreliable their assessments were. There was a risk for citizens of fragmentation and capture by conspiracy theorists within this brave new world, but those risks were often overstated and given far more attention than the parallel problems of the legacy media – everything from concentration of ownership to the way in which political journalists work hand-in-glove with politicians, to the utter contempt in which many journalists held their audience. Without social media, the independents could not have the success they had, and in a study by RMIT that looked at the way in which Monique Ryan's campaign in Kooyong used social media, the authors noted that not only did 'Dr Monique Ryan's historic win in the federal seat of Kooyong [mark] a rupture in the electoral status-quo, suggesting a waning influence of legacy media in shaping the election result', but that 'Josh Frydenberg's extensive billboard advertising and generally supportive stories published by News Corp media were no match for the community-focused social media campaign led by Dr Ryan and her supporters.'

Change happens fast, and then it happens slowly, and while the full ramifications of the 2022 election will only reveal themselves by and by, there are some lessons we can take away from what we already know.

We must stop using the language of the pre-internet age to describe our politics: words and phrases like 'the mainstream media', the 'two-party system', the 'major' and 'minor' parties, the idea of a 'hung parliament', let alone concepts like 'horserace' politics. All of these speak to a mindset and a politics that no longer exist, and we must break the habits of language that summon their ghosts to haunt us. This language leads us into an idea of political practice that is confrontational, team-based and competitive, rather than allowing for the possibility of a more deliberative and co-operative approach. Democracy is more usefully conceived of as happening in a garden that needs care and cultivation than on a football field where two teams butt heads and score goals for their side. The language we use to describe the process of politics should better reflect this sort of understanding. I mean, look at how most media have reported the arguments about climate change policy since the election (before the election, too). Almost exclusively they have focused on the politics of the issue, rather than the real world challenge of managing climate change itself. This ABC report from late July is entirely typical:

> The government can't afford to make sizeable concessions to the Greens, not least because that would cast doubt on the reliability of its word. It is also anxious to signal it is not hostage to the Greens, despite its dependence on them in the upper house when legislation is contested.
>
> Can the Greens afford to give in to the government and not oppose the bill? They would disappoint their hard-line supporters. They too, in political terms, need differentiation. But if they were to sink the legislation, they'd be accused of putting purist ideology ahead of supporting progressive policy. The Greens have quite a lot on the line in their decision.

Compare this to the way Monique Ryan explained the issue in her newsletter to the Kooyong electorate:

> The Climate Change and Energy Minister, Chris Bowen, has consulted with the members of the crossbench and I have provided some initial feedback on the bill, including the need for:
>
> - a preamble which states that we face a climate emergency which requires urgent and immediate action and commits the Australian

government to action consistent with the
Paris Agreement objective of limiting global
warming to 1.5 degrees Celsius

- the articulation of the 43% emissions reduction
target for 2030 as a floor, not a ceiling

- a ratcheting mechanism to lock in reductions
and to ensure that future targets can only be
more ambitious over time.

I will support the bill but this is only the beginning
point of my legislative agenda for urgent climate
action. In keeping with my campaign pledge to the
Kooyong community, I remain strongly committed
to introducing legislation on vehicle emissions,
which would have a significant impact on reducing
emissions from the transport sector. Legislating
fuel efficiency and emissions standards is a crucial
measure that will ensure that Australia achieves
emissions reductions much greater than 43% by
2030.

The horserace focus of the ABC article is replaced with
concrete discussion of the actual, physical problems of
climate change and how it might be addressed, and the
contrast could not be starker between the insider nature
of the old politics and the goal-focused politics of the
new. To underline that, Ryan concluded by saying, 'I will
be back in touch with regular updates and information

on how you can all be involved in seeking climate change action consistent with the scientific expert advice', and she speaks about organising community gatherings for members of her electorate, underlining again that consultation, not competition, is built into the approach the independents represent.

You could make a list of things the Albanese government has done well, and it would be of a decent length. You could also make a list of all the bad things they have done – ditto – and you could then make a judgment that *on balance* the good outweighed the bad, or vice versa. But that is precisely the wrong way to understand politics in this new era. 'Balance' is another old-media trope that doesn't serve us well in this era (if it ever did). Even Anthony Albanese acknowledged as much in his address in the Great Hall of parliament on the first sitting day: 'There's no middle path, no middle path. Make it a source of pride.' He was talking about Constitutional recognition of First Nations people, and you could only hope that he would extend similar think-ing to climate change and other key issues in which incrementalism will be fatal. Only in a world of horserace politics in which a governing party tries to maintain the status quo would the party in power think it was more important to honour a demonstrably inadequate election promise – the carbon target – than to offer a better target.

In the months since the election, it has become apparent that whatever improvements Labor offer in terms of governance, they remain part of the status quo. I think they have misjudged the national mood and I suspect they will pay a price at the next election, just as the Liberals did at the last one. They have fallen instantly into asserting their right to govern entirely on their own terms, and it is such an old politics. It has been simply incredible, for instance, to hear new Minister for Industry Ed Husic defending pork barrelling as something that should be handled by ministers, not bureaucrats, telling ABC Radio that 'Parliamentarians ... are up for the judgment of people every three years or so. And if they've done the wrong thing that should be done that way. I do get concerned if you just spin it all off to departmental people.'

It is a politics the country is tired of, and unless Labor recalibrate, I suspect they will be abandoned. And by recalibrate, I don't just mean change direction on a policy here and there because they are being pressured, as they did with the Covid leave payment (as welcome as that was). I mean recalibrate their entire approach to governing so that it recognises the stark reality that the majority that gives them power in the parliament is not backed up with an electoral majority of similar power in the country itself. Many argue that the raw numbers of the primary vote are irrelevant in a preferential system such as Australia's, but however you look at it, whatever excuses you make for Labor's primary vote being as low as it is, the truth is that close to a third of the country rejected the two-party system and wanted a parliament in which a wider range of voices was heard.

To put it another way, Labor can't rely simply on being a better alternative to the LNP: they must do politics differently. The lesson the rise of the independents and the consolidation of the Greens' position has taught us is that there is a power in the country that is prior to that of the status quo, and that is the power of the people. That power may coincide broadly with many aspects of business-as-usual politics, but it represents a major difference in approach. The expectations of the electorate are not the expectations of any given party. Again, this is not some sort of radical desire to up-end the entire basket of knitting but a desire that the wall between insiders and outsiders be far more permeable. Even among the government's allies in the community, expectations have been raised, and there is little patience with the idea that Labor should be left alone to govern according to some ill-defined mandate. This isn't necessarily support for independents per se, but it is a recognition that they can serve the purpose of placing pressure on incumbents, acting as a third force that expands the range of possible outcomes. Support for the Albanese government is likely a mile wide and an inch deep.

The new third force within the electorate aren't swinging voters in the traditional sense, switching their vote between Labor and the LNP. They are, rather, an empowered middle that will vote tactically to try to engineer a progressive outcome, even if that means voting for independents. Again, we need to take a beat and recognise the new forces that are at work here and how badly our usual frames of reference capture the way in which things have changed. 'Swinging voters' is another old-politics concept we need to abandon.

The two-party mindset has gone, its logic no longer holds. This is being expressed though the ballot box, but also through the volatility of social media that works outside the carefully constructed narratives of the handmaiden legacy media. This volatility doesn't mean social media is any less thoughtful – often the opposite is true, providing as it does open access to expertise not always given voice in the legacy media. But it does operate differently, thinking out loud in real time, organising itself outside the front page and six o'clock news bulletin mindset, and it inevitably gets messy. Social media angers the legacy media precisely because it rides roughshod over their sacred framings and theories of civility, but in the end, that is their problem. They can dismiss users of social media as sewer rats and the like – as leading journalists have – but in the end such insults are full of sound and fury and signify nothing except their own irrelevance.

The new elevated middle of our political landscape isn't necessarily anarchic. In many ways it is conservative. But relative to other mainstream formations, it is a force for change in how we do politics. The independents elected in 2022 come to the parliament without the vested interests of the insiders they sit beside, the members of the parties who trace a career path from student politics through jobs as staffers to ministers and shadow ministers, and into parliament via safe seats that all but guarantee them a level of employment security most people under 40 can no longer rely on – thanks to political decisions taken by people like them – and then onto the Elysian Fields of the lobbying landscape in the political afterlife. The contrast with the independents could not be starker. They come to parliament not on the back of loyalty to a party, but loyalty to a community. They aren't relying on politics to provide their life with its whole meaning, let alone their entire career. They can come in, set some goals, do some good, and then go back to the legal firm or the doctor's surgery. It is a politics that is contingent but focused.

Is this good for democracy?

Undoubtedly. It ruptures the structures in which complacency and corruption grow. It undermines the cosy habits of the status quo. It reminds the establishment that governing legitimacy comes from the *demos*, the people, not the elites. It echoes the essence of self-rule the Greeks were trying to achieve though sortition and democracy itself. It is a landmine under the oligarchical mindset that is the inevitable endpoint of two-party politics. The logic of this formation flies in the face of party logic and heralds a new sort of practical, ends-focused politics. It doesn't describe the entire body of citizens, but it does characterise a significant, central section of it. It is a statistical centre, too, not an ideological one, and 2022 was the first time ever this middle got above 30 per cent of the national vote. These are the knowledge class. The mainstream outsiders. They are thoughtful, engaged, discerning and independent.

Perhaps we have become a more individualistic society and can't invest our entire identity in the pre-digested ideologies of the so-called major parties, of labour versus capital, of rich versus poor, of blue versus red. And yet, we do not want to dispense with the idea of government, let alone community and other forms of solidarity. Organisations like the Voices Of movement reflect a new point of balance between individual needs and the needs of community. We did not subscribe to Scott Morrison's radical idea of a lack of trust in government (especially if it is to be replaced with a trust in God), but we require more personal involvement in the role government plays, something beyond a two-party system. We are normalising the idea that the crossbench should play a more prominent role.

We want a system of government that recognises our individual wants and needs, but that also performs its collective role in managing the risks that affect all of us. Pandemic and climate change bring home to us the indivisibly collective nature of the problems that confront us and so we recognise that our personal integrity means nothing unless the collective nature of society holds together. In a sense we are brought back to the fundamental problem of survival itself, to the reason tribes, communities, societies and nations form in the first place – to bring the power of collective risk-management to bear on matters that no individual can manage by themselves.

The broad shape of three-party politics, as I've defined it, is still developing, and a full assessment must be withheld until at least the next election. If Labor can produce a successful term of government, they could consolidate their parliamentary majority, but it is important to recognise that that can only occur if the independents continue to hold the Liberal Party at bay. The Coalition has fallen into a shambles they are unlikely to emerge from anytime soon, and indications are that they will double down on more extreme right-wing positions, in a version of what has happened to the Republican Party in the United States. Labor will continue to consolidate the space vacated by the Coalition, allowing them to build a new settlement between capital and labour, and we are seeing this in policies as various as high-earner tax cuts, the retention of the Fair Work Commission, and the continued enforcement of 'mutual obligations' on those seeking work though a privatised job network, with no increase in unemployment benefits. As Guy Rundle has written, 'a Labor government is going to argue for a more generous treatment of workers by capital, and may shift regulations as such, but it is not going to make any changes that would shift structural power relations even slightly.'

It is unclear which direction the independents will lean – the signs are mixed – and it is in the nature of their solo status that, despite broad agreement in key areas, each will respond differently to challenges that arise. This diversity is to be welcomed rather than feared. Key is that they maintain their close ties to their communities and resist being dragged into the status quo of the old political class so that this latest experiment in Australian political practice has a chance to put us on a new and more democratic path.

We will learn much about our democracy, and

ourselves, as we move towards the referendum on a First Nations Voice to parliament, and the final form it takes will be less important than the integrity of the process that gets us to that result, whatever it is. It is a huge challenge to the idea of what an Australian state even means.

In the end, it's climate, stupid.

Climate change presents us with a social and political challenge of such magnitude that incremental, business-as-usual politics won't be enough. Individual responses will not work. Extractive capitalism will not work. The power of the status quo to resist reform remains strong, but it is up against the ability of the planet to sustain life, and who do you think is going to win? If we reach a point of collapse – we can feel its hot breath on our necks already – without creating the democratic buttresses to bear equally the burdens that will inevitably arise, all we will be left with is an authoritarianism that will impose climate controls on us. In other words, a form of eco-fascism. I can imagine critics scoffing at this, and saying that I am exaggerating, but there is simply too much evidence of authoritarianism emerging around the world to take any comfort in assurances that eco-fascism isn't a real possibility. Recognising this is not a negative approach to take, but a positive necessity.

The 2022 election gave us a reprieve. It gave us a new government, more focused than its predecessor on addressing climate change, on the centrality of First Nations, and on the role of women, and it gave us the chance of a new way to do politics. But if the new third force of Australian politics is to mean anything beyond a fleeting feel-good moment, the new independent office bearers of the crossbench in the house and in the Senate, and the legacy parties themselves, are going to need to be far more radical than any small-l liberal, centrist positioning allows.

There is no sensible centre on a dead planet.

Climate change is coming, ready or not, and if we don't deal with it democratically, in deliberative discussions around kitchen tables and in our houses of parliament, then all that will be left is authoritarianism. Because we are going to have to deal with it.

Our transformation from a competitive, two-party system of democracy into a fully-fledged system of community engagement and deliberation will not be easy, but it has been given an enormous boost by the Voices Of movement and other forms of community politics that have emerged over the last decade. Their success in 2022 shows us that a better politics is possible if we commit ourselves to it and stop listening to the siren voices of the status quo that seek to convince us that there is no alternative.

There *is* an alternative, and it is the voices of us.

Acknowledgments

I want to pay tribute to Margo Kingston and Peter Clarke. More than any other journalist, Margo has amassed interviews with the independent candidates and the behind-the-scenes organisers, allowing them to tell their stories of this incredible community process, as well as interrogating aspects of the movement, and I could not have written this book without the archive she has created at her *No Fibs* website. Before anyone else, going back to her coverage of the Hanson phenomenon, Margo saw the importance of what was happening with the emergence of independents around the country – in fact, she predicted it in her book *Not Happy, John!* – and has been ahead of the game ever since. Peter's peerless technical skill made the podcast possible in the first place, and discussions with him helped sharpen my focus and have clarified my thinking. The *#transitzone* podcast is another vital archive that helped make the book possible and it would not exist without Peter's work. I owe them both a debt of gratitude.

I want to thank Louise Hislop for speaking with me at length and giving me an insight into the community organising that underpinned Voices Of movements across the country, and for inviting me to talk with

Voices of Warringah in the first place. Her own account of her experiences, written for *No Fibs*, is a treasure. If she is not on the next Australia Day honours list, there is something wrong with the system.

The team at NewSouth Publishing have my thanks for organising this book on a very tight deadline. Harriet McInerney and Paul O'Beirne ran the whole project with grace and aplomb. Thanks and much respect to Tricia Dearborn for her editing skills, without which my manuscript would not have passed muster.

Some of the ideas and arguments presented here were first written for other publications, most especially *Meanjin*, under the unparalleled editorship of Jonathan Green, and I extend to him my thanks and appreciation. Oliver Gray, editor of *Art of the Essay* at the *Market Herald*, has been supportive and a pleasure to work with. I want to acknowledge, too, William Forsythe's incredible work of dance, *In the Middle, Somewhat Elevated*, a title I borrowed for one of my chapters. I have received great feedback from those who subscribe to my *Future of Everything* newsletter, and I am grateful for their ongoing support. I'd especially like to recognise Noely Neate, Elana Mitchell, David Irving, Zoe Bowman, Renn Barker and @paddybts for support over many years. Discussions and exchanges with Ingrid Matthews, John Quiggin, Matthew Brown – one of my oldest friends in the world – Jane Gilmour, Hal Crawford, Margaret Simons, Tim Hollo, Paul Atkinson, Karen Barker and Paul Kildea have been a valuable source of information and clarity.

Social media, Twitter in particular, gets a lot of bad press, but we need to recognise these new forums as part of the fusion-media landscape in which politics is now conducted. Contributions made there by people like Tim Lyons, Michelle Arrow, Amy McQuire, Amy Remeikis, Margaret Morgan, Kerryn Goldsworthy, Frank Bongiorno, Paul Kidd, Ronni Salt, Denise Shrivell, Ben Raue, Kevin Bonham, David Sligar and others make it a valuable source of comment, information and fact-checking. I am grateful to be able to access their insights.

As always, infinite love and thanks go to my wife Tanya and my son Noah, without whom I would be lost. Their love and support are everything to me and they bring me joy.

Index

Index

McKenzie, Bridget 123
Macphee, Julie 47
Mahlab, Eve 47
Manne, Robert 84–85
Mansfield (VIC electorate) 28
Mathison, James 34–35, 38, 39
Meanjin 127, 129
media
    2022 election coverage 136–140, 155–156
    ABC 136, 141, 155, 194, 201
    anti-Labor bias 131–134
    'drops' and strategic leaks 134–136, 140
    independent news media publishers 147
    legacy 92, 143, 148, 199, 200, 206
    political 127–148
    reform 145–148
    vested interests 133
Melleuish, Greg 86, 88
Menadue, John 108–109
Menzies, Robert 47, 53, 84, 132, 133
Michael West Media 147
Mirabella, Sophie 1, 39
The Monthly 54, 147, 195
Morrison, Scott 3–5, 13, 41, 48, 50–51, 57, 64, 66, 70, 105–106, 114–124, 142, 165
    'captain's picks' 50–51
    government 114–124, 135
    Hawaiian holiday 6, 115
    multiple ministerial portfolios 124
    Pentecostalism 48, 57, 101
    personal staff numbers 117
    style of prime ministership 4–6
    Turnbull leadership spill 41
Murphy, Katharine 196
Murugappan family 7

neoliberalism 20, 21, 65–69, 74, 81, 82, 85, 89, 95, 103, 115, 167
News Corporation 134, 136, 140, 142–143, 145, 200
    call for Royal Commission into 134, 143
Nine Entertainment 133
    vested interests 138–139
North Sydney (NSW electorate) 48, 53, 55, 174
    Voices Of 146
Not Happy, John! (book) 30, 212

Oakeshott, Rob 97
One Nation 59, 87, 88, 97, 157

Pagone, Tony 120
Palmer, Clive 170, 172
pandemic *see* Covid-19
Paper Emperors (book) 131
Parkinson, Martin 109
Paterson (NSW electorate) 58
Pearls and Irritations (website) 108–109
Pearson, Noel 88
Pengilly, Kurt 35
Phelps, Kerryn 41–43, 53, 55, 97
Plibersek, Tanya 194
Polanyi, Karl 151
pork barrelling 121–122, 204
Port Arthur massacre 83
Priestly, Rob 54
privatisation 65, 66, 69, 115–116, 209
*PS Media 147
Purple Sage project 19–21, 85

Question Time 113

Raue, Ben 177, 214
Reason Party 54
Reed, Anthony 42–43, 55
republican debate 79, 80, 85, 90

Rickard, John 73
Ridge, Kathryn 37
Rigged: How networks of powerful mates rip off everyday Australians (book) 109
Robodebt 119–120
Rocher, Alan 97
Rolden, Clara Williams 36
Rowland, Michelle 143
Royal Commissions
    into aged care 120–121
    into the banking industry 124
Rudd, Kevin 33, 34, 98, 134, 195–196
Ryan, Monique 6, 48, 51, 53, 155, 189, 199–202
    Federal Court challenge 166

Sales, Leigh 194
Salusinszky, Imre 86
same-sex marriage 70, 162–163
    2017 plebiscite 3, 99
Samuel, Graeme 109
The Saturday Paper 56, 147
Saul, John Ralston 117–118
Say Yes 30–31
Scamps, Sophie 6, 48, 51–53, 55
Scarlett, Leonie 52
secret ballot 79, 81, 180
Schultz, Julianne 69, 108
Scott, Pennie 54
Sharkie, Rebekha 157
Sharma, Dave 36, 41, 141
Shields, Bevan 139
Shrivell, Denise 53–54, 146–147, 214
Simons, Margaret 54–55, 127, 143, 147, 213
sortition 183–187, 207
Speers, David 46
Spender, Allegra 6, 48, 51, 53, 55
sports grant rorts 122
status quo 131, 142–143, 197
    automatic stabilisers of 107–111, 154

CPSIA information can be obtained
at www.ICGtesting.com
Printed in the USA
BVHW042001291122
653038BV00002B/15